The Retrospective Handbook

Handbook

A guide for agile teams

Patrick Kua

Foreword by Diana Larsen

The Retrospective Handbook
A guide for agile teams

Patrick Kua

This book is for sale at
http://leanpub.com/the-retrospective-handbook

This version was published on 2013-01-26

ISBN 1480247871

Contents

Foreword by Diana Larsen

Over fifteen years ago, Norm Kerth (author of *Project Retrospectives: A Handbook for Team Reviews*) asked me to lead a retrospective for a team. He was acting as interim manager for the project which made him ineligible for the role of neutral facilitator - he knew he had opinions about the project and wanted to contribute them. We'd met through a mutual friend, and he had learned that I had experience with meeting facilitation and helping technical teams improve their work processes. I felt honoured that he asked me and curious about his format. He gave me an unpublished manuscript and said, "Read this...you'll be fine." I read it, we designed a three-day meeting, and the resulting retrospective went so well that he included a blow-by-blow description of it in his book.

That was my first introduction to project team retrospectives. It changed the course of my career and my life. Over the last fifteen years, I've collaborated with Norm, Esther Derby, Deborah Lavell, Gerhard Ackermann, Linda Rising, Boris Gloger, Rachel Davies, Charlotte Malther, Ainsley Nies, Josef Scherer, George Dinwiddie, and a host of other excellent retrospective leaders to establish the annual international "Retrospective Facilitators Gathering" and co-authored (with Esther) Agile Retrospectives: Making Good Teams Great. The movement to adopt Agile approaches to software development gave teams the opportunity to continuously improve their methods, practices, processes, and teamwork throughout the project, not just at the end. Esther and I offered workshops in leading Agile retrospectives at the end of iterations and releases to scores of people worldwide, and we weren't the only ones. Retrospectives became an accepted part of the cannon of Agile practices.

Getting to know Patrick Kua was one of the delights associated with the 2007 Retrospective Facilitators Gathering (RFG, for short) in Phoenix, Arizona. Pat brought a high degree of creative energy and enthusiasm to retrospective leadership. I enjoyed hearing about his experiences, his designs, and his innovations for the practice. I began following his blog posts and gained an even greater respect for his skills as an Agile coach. We looked for opportunities to collaborate on conference sessions. Over time, he became a leading thinker and writer about designing and facilitating highly effective retrospectives.

In 2006, when Esther and I published *Agile Retrospectives*, we used the term "retrospective leader" rather than "facilitator" to describe the role. At the time, in general, development team members, team leads, player-coaches, and scrum masters held low opinions of "touchy-feely," "group process," and words like "fluffy bunny" and "facilitator" that accompanied them. Since then, the role of a meeting facilitator and the skill of facilitation have gained recognition as an essential skill for team leaders and team members.

In this book, Pat underscores that awareness. He includes many aspects of retrospective facilitation that

Esther and I left out, delving deeply into preparation and follow through, various types of retrospectives (he calls them flavours), common retrospective smells (to expand into another sense), retrospectives with distributed teams, and how to keep them fresh. He also provides pointers to group process activities and resources for improving one's skills as a facilitator. It is truly a soup-to-nuts compendium of the wisdom he's gained from his experiences.

As Norm introduced me to the format of retrospectives, let Pat introduce you to his perceptive, discriminating, and ingenious take on facilitating retrospectives. And I hope to meet you at an RFG someday!

- Diana Larsen

partner, FutureWorks Consulting LLC

co-author, *Agile Retrospectives: Making Good Teams Great*

co-author, *Liftoff: Launching Agile Teams & Projects*

Preface

I have fond memories of my first 'agile team' experience, mostly Extreme Programming (XP)-inspired with fortnightly planning sessions, with frequent releases and retrospectives at the end of each iteration. We would stop for an hour each fortnight, celebrate positive aspects, and explore any issues we had at all levels: technical, team and environment. My teammates and I found that we became highly engaged because we could directly influence the way we worked and we could continue experimenting and fine-tuning our work methods as circumstances changed.

We released software into production every single fortnight. I felt so much more productive than I had in a previous job, where I had worked on a large, distributed project for a huge coproration, and had rarely heard people talk about change or improvement. The contrast between these experiences helped me to see how retrospectives create 'safe spaces' and inspired me to want to run and facilitate retrospectives.

In London I met Tim MacKinnon, another XP developer who was passionate about the retrospective practice. On one occasion, because he had no time and knew of my passion for retrospectives, he asked me to facilitate a project retrospective.

I was extremely nervous about being an 'official' facilitator for the first time and I searched desperately for a book to tell me how I could run it successfully. I wanted advice about potential traps and how best to prepare for the upcoming retrospective.

Unfortunately, I found nothing at the time and was thankful when the retrospective went successfully. Participants had raised some tough problems but people left with closure on some issues, a better shared understanding of why certain events had unfolded, and lessons to share with other project teams.

Even though this first retrospective had gone well, I felt that this was largely down to good fortune and still wished that I had had a resource offering practical advice on how to prepare for a variety of retrospective situations.

Hence this book. I hope it serves you well, as the resource I wish had existed when I first started facilitating retrospectives.

Acknowledgements

This book would not exist without the countless organisations and people for whom I facilitated retrospectives, or without the countless teams where I participated in retrospectives of every kind. All experiences (good and bad) contributed to the advice I give in this book and validated through exchanges with other passionate facilitators. I can highly recommend attending the yearly Retrospective Facilitators' Gathering to meet more passionate facilitators.

I am grateful for the feedback on early drafts from the following people: Todd Anderson, Ilias Bartolini, Patrick Downey, Susmita Maharana, Jennifer Smith, Tom Sulston, Francisco Trindade, May Ping Xu, Jason Yip.

I wish to thank the team behind leanpub for the platform they created. The platform allowed me to focus more on content instead of fussing over formatting.

Finally, thanks to both Esther Derby and Diana Larsen, who were very direct with a recommendation that I source a professional copy-editor. The book definitely needed it at that stage. My thanks to Tom Duckering, who put me in touch with Angela Potts of Virtual Editor[1], a wonderful copy-editor whom I collaborated with remotely. Angela did a wonderful job turning the raw text into a much better book that I hope you will enjoy reading.

---

[1]http://www.virtualeditor.co.uk/

Acknowledgments

Introduction

With more organisations choosing agile methodologies to deliver software, more teams are picking up the practice of agile retrospectives. You may be working on one of these teams already and regularly use agile retrospectives to seek continuous improvement; if not, your team may find the agile retrospective practice beneficial to your work.

The Retrospective Handbook is intended as an aid to running more effective retrospectives and to complement existing books on retrospectives. It is important to use a good variety of activities to make an engaging retrospective, but this handbook intentionally focuses less on listing activities in favour of addressing the practical challenges you are likely to encounter when running retrospectives.

The contents of this book reflect advice I have been asked for time and again by people interested in the retrospective practice. Some questions came from newcomers to the agile retrospective practice, who had problems making retrospectives useful, while other questions came from retrospective facilitators keen to hear alternative approaches to common problems. *The Retrospective Handbook* also contains advice on working with seasoned agile teams, and explores ways of changing the retrospective practice to be even more engaging and insightful.

Some of the questions I answer in this book include:

- What is the Retrospective Prime Directive and why should I care?
- How can I improve how I facilitate retrospectives?

- How important is an independent facilitator?
- How do I run a distributed retrospective effectively?
- What different types of retrospectives do people run?
- What can I do to keep retrospectives fresh?
- How do we make sure that we get results from the retrospective?

The answers to these questions and many more are drawn not only from my own experience with the retrospective practice, helping clients and teams overcome frustrations and puzzles they faced, but also from numerous other retrospective facilitators who have passed on their insights and wisdom. I hope *The Retrospective Handbook* helps you to increase the effectiveness of your retrospectives and enables your team to go from strength to strength for years to come.

1 Retrospective Fundamentals

1.1 A Short History of Retrospectives

Norm Kerth first published his ideas on the retrospective practice in his 2001 book, *Project Retrospectives: A Handbook for Team Reviews* [KERTH]. The book describes retrospectives as:

> A ritual gathering of a community at the end of the project to review the events and learn from the experience. No one knows the whole story of a project. Each person has a piece of the story. The retrospective ritual is the collective telling of the story and mining the experience for wisdom.

Kerth's book describes how retrospectives differ from 'Project Post Mortems' and 'Lessons Learnt' sessions with a particular focus on taking positive action and acting as a catalyst for change. At around the same time, a number of authors published the Agile Manifesto[1] as a way of rallying people to adopt lightweight methodologies. These new agile methodologies and approaches made learning and communication primary concerns. One of the principles

---

[1]http://agilemanifesto.org/

of the Agile Manifesto aligns very well with the practice of retrospectives:

> At regular intervals, the team reflects on how to become more effective, then tunes and adjusts its behaviour accordingly.

The agile community started to embrace the key idea of the retrospective practice. Agile teams saw that they didn't need to wait until the end of a project to run a retrospective and began running them at the end of each iteration. Instead of running retrospectives every three, six or twelve months, teams ran retrospectives as frequently as every week, or at least every month. By stepping back and reflecting on current situations, teams realised value immediately by applying recommendations whilst the project was in flight, rather than at the end.

The following table highlights practices and principles that align well with the spirit of retrospectives.

Methodology	Practice or Principle
Extreme Programming	Fix XP When It Breaks
Scrum	Sprint Retrospective practice
Crystal Clear	Reflective Improvement
Adaptive SW Development	Learn
Lean SW Development	Amplify Learning
Kanban	Improve Collaboratively
DSDM Atern	Timebox Close-Out
RUP	Adapt the Process

Reflecting over a shorter period of time, one to four weeks instead of three to twelve months changed the nature of these meetings. Kerth wrote about taking several days to fully reflect over a project, but looking back over a significantly shorter period, at the end of an iteration rather than an entire project, reduces the time needed to conduct an agile retrospective. Instead of project retrospectives lasting several days, agile retrospectives only take an hour or two to run. In response to these shorter meetings, sometimes called 'Heartbeat Retrospectives', Esther Derby and Diana Larsen published the *Agile Retrospectives: Making Good Teams Great* [DERBY]. This book provided a significant contribution to the retrospective community, providing a more relevant framework for agile teams and an even wider set of exercises for people to try out.

1.2 The Key Questions

At the heart of the agile retrospective is the idea of looking for lessons learnt and methods of improvement. It is with this agile mindset of constantly learning, inspecting and adapting, that we ask: What did we do well? What did we do less well? What still puzzles us?

We ask **'What went well?'** so that we can explore and celebrate the good practices the team are doing. Constant celebration of success imparts energy to the team, driving them to experiment further. Recognising success also provides important positive feedback on any changes the team trialled, further cementing those changes into place.

Focusing on success helps team members to explore other ways to amplify already successful changes.

We ask **'What went less well?'** to jointly agree the pain points the team may have experienced. Only by exploring the background to problems that have arisen, rather than the symptoms each individual may have seen, can teams develop a shared understanding of the issues at hand. Only with a shared understanding can teams move forward productively to choose solutions that the team trials.

We ask **'What still puzzles us?'** to help team members address issues that don't fall under the previous two categories. Sometimes agile iterations or sprints move so fast that people don't have chance to ask about something that just puzzles them. There may be a revelation that no one else knows the answer either. If we skip this question, we lose the opportunity to learn surprising insights people may have.

1.3 A Simple Framework

While the key questions appear straightforward enough, you may consider using the simple framework outlined in *Agile Retrospectives* [DERBY] for more impact. It is effective for both planning and running retrospectives. The retrospective framework consists of five phases:

1. Set the Stage

Introduce the purpose of the retrospective and help establish the focus for this retrospective (eg. the last week, or the last two weeks). If there have been previous retrospectives related to the same project, this is a good point to review actions taken as a result of those retrospectives, connecting them with this retrospective. This phase is also useful for testing the comfort level, or safety and engagement level of the group. It also presents the ideal opportunity to introduce the Prime Directive[2].

2. Gather Data

This stage is for collecting facts or key memories that stand out in the minds of the team members. It is important for the facilitator to help collect sufficient information from all participants to generate a common understanding of what happened during the focus period.

3. Generate Insights

This phase is where the team focuses on interpreting the data gathered in the previous phase, perhaps exploring why certain events happened or the impact that they had on the team and the project. Facilitators work to ensure that blame is not apportioned to any one individual. The team strives to discover the possible causes and effects before identifying possible solutions or improvements.

---

[2]http://www.retrospectives.com/pages/retroPrimeDirective.html

4. Decide What to Do

The team have now brainstormed a large possible list of things to try. Attempting to tackle all of them often results in only a handful of them being done. During this phase, participants narrow down the list of viable alternatives and agree as a group which actions they will try.

5. Close the Retrospective

The possibility of change and a plan of action feels exciting. This phase helps teams recognise a successful outcome, leaving them more enthused to make change happen.

You may be tempted to skip the five phases. Avoid skipping any phase if you can. Teams that skip a phase tend to suffer with poor-quality discussions and less effective changes, or sometimes no change whatsoever! I think this framework works because it caters to people's tendency to have conversations at a different pace. Using the framework ensures that everyone progresses at the same time. Any changes are more likely to succeed because everyone is part of the process.

Without the framework, there is a danger of people jumping to conclusions and recommending an action before everyone has a shared understanding of the issues. This action will almost always be suboptimal or address the wrong problem. Chris Argyris, one of the founders of organisational psychology, introduced the concept of the **Ladder of Inference** to explain how people process information. You can find a more detailed explanation of this in Peter Senge's *The Fifth Discipline: The Art & Practice of the Learning Organization* [SENGE].

The Ladder of Inference

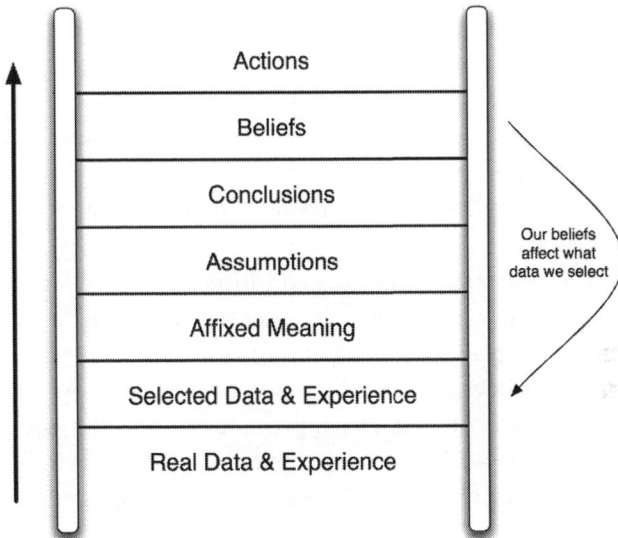

The Ladder of Inference

Argyris described this model about the way that people behave (actions) and what factors drive those behaviours. I have interpreted his description in a diagram (above). The ladder attempts to explain the way that we interact with the world.

At the bottom of the ladder, we *experience some event*, eg. 'Bob opened a window to freshen the room and to get rid of the smell of stale milk that had been left out overnight.' Each individual will interpret this event selectively, mostly subconsciously, based on their current beliefs, and so each *recalls the experience differently*, eg. 'Bob left that window open.' We quickly move to *affix meaning* to the events, eg. 'Bob made that room draughty,' often applying unchecked *assumptions*, eg. 'Bob's trying to make me sick.' This inevitably leads us to *jump to a conclusion*, eg. 'Bob doesn't like me.' These conclusions further our *beliefs*, which feed back to inform the basis of our actions.

The problem is that we tend to climb this ladder so quickly in our minds that we don't even realise we are doing it. It may sound extreme for someone to conclude that, 'Bob doesn't like me' based on his once opening the window, but it does happen and shows how easily a working relationship can be put in jeopardy. Here's a real example of someone climbing rapidly up the ladder of inference:

> I was working on a client project in a remote area of England. The client had a long history but had almost no internal management or facilities staff. As a result, when a new consultant turned up one day, they were asked to get directly involved with helping staff to rearrange their desks. The consultant set out with the new seating plan in hand and helped

people to find their new location and packed and unpacked boxes for them (*real event*). At a certain point in the day, one permanent staff member suddenly went ballistic and screamed abuse at the consultant for several minutes before running out of steam. The permanent staff member thought the consultant was responsible for making everyone move desks (*selected data*) and saw the consultant's cheerful attitude as smugness (*assumption*). He seemed to have formed the *belief* that the consultant was interfering and working against the permanent staff and so flew off the handle (*action*). Naturally, in his ignorance, the consultant was completely baffled by what had just happened.

The ladder of inference explains why people may already be itching to take an action, but often one person's chosen action addresses the wrong problem for a group as a whole.

It is the job of the facilitator to remind participants that the simple retrospective framework is there for a reason. To get maximum effect from the retrospective, everyone should progress through the five phases at the same pace.

1.4 Where to Find Activities

Activities are facilitated exercises conducted during a retrospective. Each activity may take only a minute or two, or much longer, depending on its purpose and team-member participation. An example activity is the 'Safety Check', where the facilitator polls people anonymously to gauge the level of 'safety'. A low safety result implies that important information is probably hidden, while a high result implies a lot of trust between participants. If you have facilitated or participated in a retrospective, you probably already know a number of activities you could run.

If you are new to retrospectives, this book equips you with a basic set of activities to run. Resources for a richer set of retrospective activities are provided in Appendix A. I chose to avoid listing activities here in order to focus on other equally important aspects of the retrospective practice. A diverse range of activities is also available on the internet because many members of the agile community share and learn from each other. Kerth's *Project Retrospectives* [KERTH] and Derby and Larsen's *Agile Retrospectives* [DERBY] are good starting points.

1.5 The Importance of the Prime Directive

In *Project Retrospectives*, Kerth introduced the Prime Directive, a statement intended to help set the stage for the retrospective. The Prime Directive states:

> 'Regardless of what we discover, we understand and truly believe that everyone did the

best job he or she could, given what was known at the time, his or her skills and abilities, the resources available, and the situation at hand.'

In my view, every retrospective should start with the Prime Directive being read out, exactly as it has been worded. I know some agile teams that regularly run retrospectives and choose to skip it in favour of delving into the other phases, but in my experience, this tends to result in less valuable retrospective outputs.

I remember going to see Kerth speak on the origins of the Prime Directive at a Retrospective Facilitator's Gathering. He spoke about why he thought it was really important. He described how he had tried to use a variety of statements before eventually settling on the current version of the directive because it proved to be the most effective. Kerth found that when teams skipped the Prime Directive, the overall quality of the retrospective was significantly diminished.

This is backed up by my own experience. I have experimented by running retrospectives without referring to the Prime Directive, or by trying a shorter, simplified version and I found that retrospectives that started with the Prime Directive turn out better. I believe this has to do with the *Pygmalion* effect; a kind of self-fulfilling prophecy where other people's expectations lead a person to behave and achieve in ways that confirm those expectations. It states that people tend to do better when treated as if they are capable of success.

What is the *Pygmalion* effect? - First published in 1968 and updated in 1992, researchers Robert Rosenthal and Lenore Jacobson set up an experiment involving students and teachers [ROSEN]. At the start of a school year, teachers were asked to give each student the Test of General Ability (TOGA), designed to measure IQ. The researchers then gave the teachers a list of students whose test results showed they were academic bloomers and probably the crème de la crème. Unbeknownst to the teachers, the list of students was a random selection made by the researchers from across all 18 classes. At the end of the school year, all the students were retested and those that had been 'highlighted' as academic bloomers demonstrated a significant increase in TOGA scores compared to those who had not been highlighted. Although there are claims that their research method appeared flawed [ELASH], its powerful story is heavily cited and findings repeated in different environments.

I believe the reason the Prime Directive is so successful is that it unwittingly taps into this *Pygmalion* effect. Instead of the weaker notion of 'let's imagine', the words 'we understand and truly believe' are essential to the retrospective. Likewise for 'everyone did the best job he or she could', which could easily be watered down.

This advice is true for agile teams running heartbeat retrospectives: start the meeting by reading out the Prime Directive. Whoever reads it out should do so as enthusiastically as possible and, even better, leave it hanging in the room to give participants a visible reminder of the statement's powerful potential.

1.6 The Right Context for Retrospectives

Remember that the retrospective ritual is just a tool, and all tools provide the most value when applied in the right context. There are times where retrospectives provide little value for the time invested and you might want to use a different tool. For me, there are two key factors that drive the potential impact of retrospectives: team dynamics and the environment.

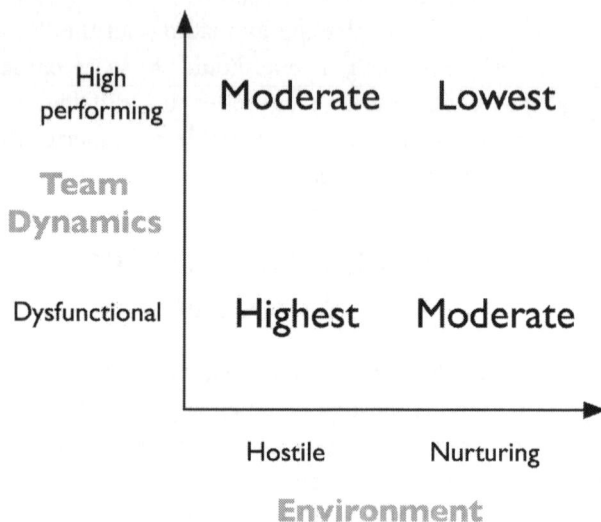

A model depicting retrospective impact

The Effect of Team Dynamics

I often hear from high-performing teams that they do not feel the need to run regular retrospectives. While I am inclined to agree, most teams are not as high performing as they think (see Illusory superiority[3] or the Dunning-Kruger effect[4]). High-performing teams distinguish themselves from dysfunctional teams through strong relationships; they understand each other's strengths, weaknesses, and

---

[3]http://en.wikipedia.org/wiki/Illusory_superiority
[4]http://en.wikipedia.org/wiki/Dunning%E2%80%93Kruger_effect

demonstrate mutual respect.

The high-performing team faces tough issues head on, working its way through disagreements to keep working relationships intact. A high-performing team suggests and implements improvements without waiting for a formal meeting. It takes action to mitigate its risks before risks become issues, helping the team to deliver with minimal effort.

High-performing teams depend less on the retrospective practice because they tap into alternative behaviours that already focus on improvement. Individuals in high-performing teams are often self-empowered and take action early, preventing issues from escalating. Retrospectives still have their place, but these teams depend less on the practice.

At the other end of the spectrum sit dysfunctional teams who typically exhibit an absence of trust, fear of conflict, lack of commitment, avoidance of accountability and inattention to results [LENCI]. By their nature, dysfunctional teams cannot address issues directly. These teams will often ignore topics that need addressing, or their conversations escalate into arguments that result in a solution not readily accepted by all. Risks quickly turn into issues, and team members wait for others to deal with problems in the hope it doesn't end up with them.

Retrospectives offer the most value for teams in this situation. A well-planned and properly facilitated retrospective creates a safe atmosphere to address issues that would otherwise be ignored. Facilitated discussions reveal the root issues, and often work at addressing team issues as much as project-related issues. Teams that are in the early stages of the their development, forming, storming and norming [TUCKM] will benefit the most.

The Effect of the Environment

Another dimension that affects the value of the retrospective practice is the environment where the team works. By environment, I mean the organisation, the culture, and the physical space that the team works in, as these often drive the behaviour and dictate communication structure even more than team dynamics.

Many organisations where I have worked could be described as more hostile than nurturing. By 'hostile' environment, I mean one where protecting the status quo is valued more than seeking and implementing improvements. In these environments, individuals avoid suggesting improvements or won't try improvements without some kind of guarantee. This is because there exists a fear of failing in public or of a consequent reprimand. Retrospectives are most powerful in these environments, because they explicitly create a safe space for people to talk openly about issues and where teams can commit to taking explicit action for improvement.

'Nurturing' environments need the retrospective practice less because they are quick to embrace failure and openly reward teams who learn from failed experiments. Because there is no fear of failure in nurturing environments, they foster an innovative attitude, where constant improvement is not only tolerated but expected from everyone all the time. Hierarchy is disregarded in these environments when it comes to suggestions and action for improvement is favoured and rewarded.

Retrospectives have less impact in nurturing environments because individuals are more likely to suggest and implement improvements without the need for a special meeting, and without the need for an entire team to be involved. Even so, while the nurturing environment does not rely on retrospectives as the sole mechanism for improvement, they can gain many benefits from holding them. Retrospectives offer the opportunity to bring a team together to create a fuller picture that would not exist without everyone's contributions, and so new insights and suggestions are raised.

1.7 Complementary Improvement Practices

The retrospective is an important tool in the bag of agile practices when you are looking for ways to inspect and adapt; it is not the only one. Here is a list of related improvement practices worth considering.

- **Kaizen** - Is the Japanese term borrowed from the lean manufacturing industry to represent continuous and incremental improvement. Kaizen is more of a mindset and culture than a specific method. Teams that adopt kaizen naturally encourage improvements all the time.

- **Quality Circles** - Created by Kaoru Ishikawa in 1962, Quality Circles typically involve a small group of 6-9 people, generally working in the same area or business unit and empowered by management to resolve work-related issues. A Quality Circle meeting typically takes an hour and focuses on a series of steps including problem identification, problem selection, problem analysis, solution brainstorming, agreeing on the best solution, and creating a potential implementation plan to present to management to get support and agreement.

- **After-Action Review** - This structured review technique was introduced by the US Army in the 1970s and is now a standard procedure. The four key questions are: 'What did we set out to do?'; 'What actually happened?'; 'Why did it happen?', and 'What are we going to do next time?' These are answered by the participants and those responsible for the project or event.

2 Preparing for Retrospectives

An agile retrospective is a meeting like any other. Even though it is a relatively short meeting, usually lasting about an hour, I find that most facilitators do not set aside sufficient time from their other tasks to properly prepare for a retrospective. A lack of preparation often results in a disproportionate amount of crucial retrospective time being spent on organising materials, the room, and deciding what activities to run rather than information gathering and getting to the crux of the matter.

2.1 Set Aside Time to Prepare

The effective facilitator sets aside two blocks of preparation time. The first is to decide the purpose of the retrospective; the second is to design an agenda around it, complete with a schedule of anticipated timings.

The purpose of the retrospective is to celebrate success and look for improvements. For a heartbeat retrospective, it makes sense to focus on the events since the last retrospective; normally one or two weeks' time. You may even choose to run a 'Focused Topic Retrospective.' For example, one team I worked on ran two separate retrospectives. One week the retrospective focused on team issues, such as the process of how stories flowed and the interactions between team members. The following week's retrospective had a technical theme, bringing in just the developers to discuss technical issues surrounding the code, design and build process. Focused Topic Retrospectives are useful but I don't recommend teams running them continually.

An agenda helps a retrospective run more smoothly. An agenda includes the activities you plan to run and their sequence. Draw the agenda on a flip chart and make it visible. Making the agenda visible throughout the retrospective is useful to keep the retrospective focused. Consider how long each activity takes to run and allow enough time for group discussion as well as time for transition between activities. Ensure the accumulated time fits into the overall time you planned for the entire retrospective. Avoid rushing people through conversations or cutting short a retrospective.

2.2 Find an Appropriate Space

An effective meeting space makes a significantly positive impact on retrospectives. Consider the exercises that you plan to run and find a room that will accommodate them. Your room should be large enough for the maximum number of potential participants and it is preferable if the chairs and tables can be easily moved around. Many activities require participants to get up and move around or require break-out space, something that many standard meeting rooms are not geared towards.

Reserve the room for at least half an hour prior to the retrospective as well as for some time afterwards. Use this time to set up for the retrospective (more on that later) and to allow for previous meetings overrunning into your team's valuable discussion time.

A room that has natural daylight and fresh air is preferable as it is more likely to remain a comfortable temperature when the room is filled with participants generating ideas and suggestions. Avoid running the retrospective in the same space where everyone sits on a day-to-day basis. Something as simple as moving into a different physical location can radically help people focus their minds away from daily tasks and to start thinking about the past and potential future.

A Brazilian colleague, Lourenço Soares, experimented running retrospectives outside. He said:

> 'The team appeared more energised, had meaningful discussions and managed to clear many of the issues we were facing.'

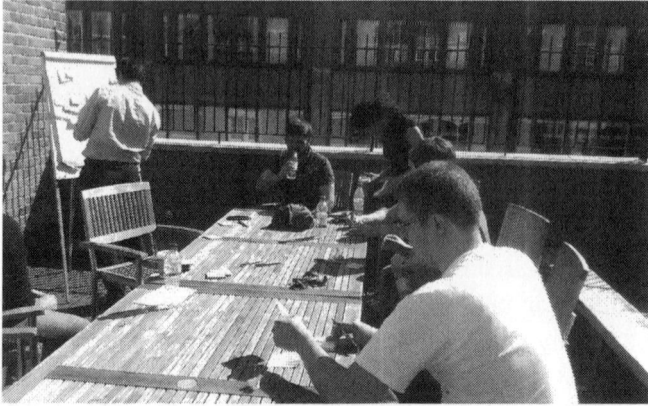

Retrospectives Outside

He offers some useful tips on planning on running meetings outside:

- **Plan for the wind** - Even a light breeze can mess up your flip charts or sticky notes. Use tape or stronger tack to keep things in place. Alternatively, look for an outdoor space that is sheltered from the elements.
- **Seek a place with shade** - The sun is great for your health but meaningful conversations can be difficult if people have to squint. Try not to accept the use of sunglasses as they can create another barrier to communication. Be aware that an hour's exposure to the sun can lead to sunburn for some.
- **Allow additional time for participants to get there** - Outside spaces are often located further away from the workplace than meeting rooms, so allow 'travel'

time and avoid inviting people back to back with another meeting as that will inevitably delay your start.

2.3 Choose the Right Materials

After working with many other facilitators, I started to realise how the right materials make such a difference to the safety, execution and wrapping up of an agile retrospective.

Prefer Marker Pens

As participants make written contributions during a retrospective, it is important that these are as legible as possible. A retrospective encourages more pairs of eyes to see all the data. If the data isn't easy to read, then it reduces the chance of someone finding a link or relationship that the rest of the group had been unaware of. Other than giving prompts such as, 'Take your time writing' or 'Please write clearly for others', there is little that the facilitator can do to control the quality of someone else's handwriting. What the facilitator can control, however, are the pens and papers that people use.

Make sure that participants write using a marker pen instead of an ordinary ballpoint pen. Markers tend to have thicker tips and use more ink than their ballpoint alternatives, which significantly improves visibility, especially when participants are sitting across the room from each other, or from the wall where you intend to display activity output. Items written in marker pen also tend to turn out better in digital photographs, as illustrated by the picture below.

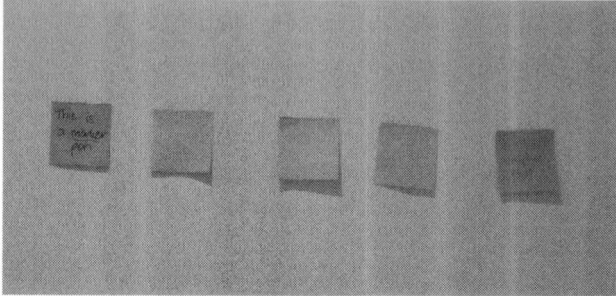

Marker pen visibility (left) versus ballpoint pen visibility (right)

Sharpie[1] is one reliable, commonly used marker brand, but, like many marker pens, its markers do have a strong chemical smell that some participants may find offensive. Browse around your local stationer and trial several brands before settling on one.

Staying with the theme of legibility, be sure to choose paper that contrasts with the pen colour so that the text stands out as much as possible. Remember that some participants may have colour-blindness. Avoid red marker on red or orange paper, for example.

Get Enough Materials for Everyone

There's nothing worse than starting an exercise only to discover there are missing materials. A well-run agile ret-

---

[1]http://www.sharpie.com/

rospective differs from other meetings in that participants contribute simultaneously wherever possible. Instead of a central scribe, everyone writes down their own input, in silence, at the same time. Once everyone has finished writing, you collect up their stickies and read the data to the whole team as you post them on the wall or flip chart. You can also ask the group to suggest where they feel that data should be grouped. Group related items to reduce duplication and seek themed clusters before using the clusters to drive more discussion. This technique also prevents 'Group Think'[2] since everyone works on their own to begin with. The result is a wider variety of input from many perspectives, which leads to a higher probability of gaining different insights.

A prerequisite for this is having sufficient materials for each participant. Consider how you will run each exercise and determine whether participants will be able to capture their thoughts immediately, or will have to wait until they are asked by the facilitator.

Consider Office Policies

A great facilitator makes the retrospective as engaging as possible by adorning the room with the retrospective outputs. The output from each exercise is put on display by the facilitator to act as a visual reference for later exercises. Displaying output in this way can help to form links between concepts previously discussed, or to trigger

---

[2]http://en.wikipedia.org/wiki/Groupthink

an insight that applies across topics.

Before you get any drawing pins or sticky tape out, though, do check whether there are any rules in place that prohibit hanging anything on the room walls. There may be regulations because a room has just been redecorated or some may feel that posters and sticky notes create a less professional appearance.

Here are some of the combinations that I have used for different environments.

- **Flip chart paper and tack** - Ripping off sheets and using tack to attach them to the wall is a cheap, easy and low-ritual way to put up the exercise results. Its versatility makes it the method of choice. Flip chart sheets are easy to tear off for group work, and then easy to hang around a room with tack for people to view results. It works really well in places where you have lots of window space and where office managers don't mind what you put where. I prefer tack over tape because it tends to remove better (depending on the brand and combination used).
- **Flip chart paper and magnets** - Works brilliantly with a full sized magnetic wall but make sure that you have enough magnets at your disposal.
- **Multiple flip charts and/or movable whiteboards** - Useful in places where you are not allowed to put anything on the walls, but often requires more floor space than many meeting rooms have. Particularly useful for boardrooms, which tend to have limited wall space due to framed artworks.

- **3M sticky flip charts** - These are great for adhering to walls that are otherwise anti-stick, and they tend not to leave a mark, keeping the office manager happy. They are quick to use with a strong bond. The downsides of these sticky flip charts are that can only be used in portrait mode; you can't write or place sticky notes on the uppermost strip (where the adhesive from the previous sheet was stuck), and sheets tend to stick together when you place them on top of one another or roll them up to take away.
- **Static cling sheets** - Static cling sheets work by maintaining a degree of cling through static forces when initially put up. They tend to work well in small spaces where other alternatives aren't possible. Static cling isn't as strong as tack or tape so you can expect sheets to occasionally float down, especially under the weight of sticky notes.

Sticky Notes Versus Index Cards or Paper

One great thing about agile retrospectives is how they help to build a common story with everyone telling potentially different parts of it. Just as index cards are employed in agile projects to represent a placeholder conversation for a user story, sticky notes act as the same placeholder conversation in the retrospective. Ask participants to call out which sticky notes they would like more detail behind, or help in understanding. This reduces the amount of talking that you, as a facilitator, need to do during the retrospective.

One pitfall I want to point out here is that since sticky notes are placeholder conversations, taking photos of them may not be meaningful and fail to capture the essence of what was discussed during the retrospective. For most teams this shouldn't be a problem as heartbeat retrospectives should be vehicles to drive immediate change. For teams where external parties want a retrospective report, note that photographs may not be sufficient. I go into more depth on this in After the Retrospective.

Use a Consistent Variety of Colours

Humans are good at pattern matching. For most people, it is quicker and easier to discern colour patterns than any other. For the facilitator, colour coding is a useful tool to inspire further insights. Pick a colour scheme to accompany each of the themes that crop up in the activities, and keep colour usage consistent. If necessary, ask people to rewrite contributions that don't match. It is easy to see where a high density of one colour starts to appear and this could inspire a discussion topic that might otherwise have remained hidden.

For example, in a classic Went Well / Less Well / Puzzles brainstorm, I usually ask participants to use green sticky notes for Went Well, pink sticky notes for Less Well, and yellow sticky notes for Puzzle contributions.

Also consider using colours if you plan on using the large flip chart pages. They help to brighten up the activities and keep it more engaging. Colours also help people feel like retrospectives are different from other meetings.

Use coloured marker pens, or thick crayon sticks to add borders to flip charts.

When teams first start with retrospectives, facilitators tend to run a safety or motivation check to test how much people will contribute to the session based on their safety or motivation. Making consistent use of colours helps improve safety by increasing anonymity. Maintaining anonymity is hard for a participant if they have the only blue pen when everyone else has a black pen. This could be the case if you use different coloured paper or sticky notes and one individual has uniquely identifiable materials.

Provide enough of the same coloured pens and same coloured paper and sticky notes for everyone to write on at once. If you are using a colour co-ordinated scheme, it's especially important when moving on to the next exercise, ensure the group is moving together at the same pace. If you aren't able to obtain enough of the same materials, try to have enough of a random factor for no small minority to be easily identifiable.

Bring a Camera

Taking photos is an effective way of capturing retrospective outputs and is much quicker than transcribing each and every word written up. Embed the resulting images into the report or wiki page you write after the retrospective to enrich the reader experience. Use a good camera with image stabilisation and a large megapixel count, which help make legible images. Take a number of pictures of a flip chart, wall, or the room from different angles so you can choose the best image later.

Visit the Space in Advance

Do not assume the space will have standard equipment such as whiteboard markers, or flip chart paper. See the space for yourself. At the very least, check that all the materials exist and operate as you'd hope. Plan for pens to go dry and bring spare ones. Always bring supplies such as tack or tape to hang materials so that you don't have to resort to flipping through pages of a flip chart. Displaying materials helps participants visualise progress throughout the retrospective and is an easy way of referring back to previous points. Bring spare flip chart paper if you suspect you will run out.

2.4 Prepare the Space

You've identified your activities and collected materials for all participants. Now it's time to prepare the room. Here's how my preparation for retrospectives looked when I first started:

> I thought I was well prepared. The room had a whiteboard, and I had brought the marker pens, sticky notes and tack that I planned on using. In my eagerness to get on with the first activity, I quickly explained how the activity would run and then stood back waiting for people to participate. Then I realised that I

hadn't given them any materials to do anything with!

Avoid running retrospectives like my first one. Think about how best to keep the flow of the retrospective running smoothly, less on the logistics of room layout, distribution or allocation of materials. Arrange the chairs so that participants will see each other and also to focus on any outputs; a semicircle is good. If you have movable tables, use the entire room and arrange the chairs in a full circle around the tables. Place a pen in front of each chair, together with any materials you want participants to use to kickstart the first exercise. Distribute further materials for the next exercise as the retrospective progresses.

A room prepared to run a retrospective with markers and sticky notes laid out

Find a large flat table in an out-of-the-way, but easily accessible place. Group the materials on the table in sequential order for each activity so it's easy to retrieve. Remove any packaging and bring spare marker pens in case people run out or there is a problem with one of them.

Prepare flip charts or whiteboards in advance and hang them around the room. To prevent participants from getting distracted by what is coming, some facilitators cover pre-drawn charts with plain flip chart paper.

Ensure the room will be a comfortable temperature when people arrive and will remain so when it is full. Air-conditioning or heating systems normally take time to kick in, so the earlier you can do this the better.

If you're running a distributed retrospective, set up any video conferencing or telephone lines before the retrospective starts. Test that projectors work or, if you plan on using a computer, check that it is switched on, you are logged in and that any applications you need are installed and open. There's nothing worse that struggling with electronic devices or waiting for applications to load with everyone watching.

2.5 Right People, Right Place, Right Time

You've made your plans, collected your materials and set up the room. Now you wait. Five minutes pass. Ten minutes pass. You know this team is normally late to retrospectives, but 15 minutes is a large chunk of your allotted time. You call someone on the team, only to discover they and everyone else have been sitting in another room. You ask them to come over to this room because you've got everything set up. Then only half the team make an appearance. 'A few of the developers had to attend a design meeting with another team and the Project Manager is talking to a Senior Director,' one participant informs you.

These things happen, but whatever you do, don't allow them to become the normal course of events for a heartbeat retrospective as it will significantly diminish the value of the shared common story and the input gathered from different perspectives. Work with the team leader to identify a minimum set of participants, or at least some criteria for postponing the retrospective (eg. four out of nine members missing). Send invitations from an electronic calendar to all participants and request confirmation of attendance on the day. Work with people whose days are meeting-heavy to book time in their calendars immediately before the retrospective so that they can avoid a back-to-back meeting running into the retrospective; do this with everyone if the retrospective location is some distance away. It's really important everyone turns up on time and is ready to participate to achieve optimum effect.

On the day, use whatever communication mechanism is commonly available (eg. stand-ups) to remind everyone of the time and location of the retrospective and the expectations for everyone participating. Although the team should ideally organise itself to get to the retrospective location, you may want to employ someone to help round people up.

These actions may seem small, but each helps to set up the retrospective for maximum impact and success.

2.6 A Preparation Checklist

Use this checklist to ensure you have done enough preparation for the retrospective.

- Do you know why you're here for the retrospective?
- Do you know how many people will turn up?
- Do you have an initial plan for how it will run?
- Is there enough time to do all the exercises?
- Do you have enough materials for everyone?
- Does the space accommodate your exercises and the number of participants?
- Have invitations been sent to all participants?
- Do you have confirmation that a quorum is present?
- Have you reserved the space (including preparation and wrap-up time)?
- Have you been briefed on what might come up?
- Are you expected to do anything after the retrospective and have you got time for that (eg. write a report, distribute action items, etc).

3 Facilitating Retrospectives

A direct contributor to the effectiveness of a retrospective is the quality of the facilitator and how they facilitate the retrospective. In this chapter, I will deal with a number of a issues particularly relevant to facilitating retrospectives over other meetings. If you are unfamiliar or uneasy with facilitating, the next chapter covers advice to help you.

3.1 Independent or Non-Independent

In an ideal world, all team retrospectives would have an independent facilitator to run their retrospectives. A facilitator outside of the team maintains neutrality and prevents discussions and outcomes being unintentionally biased. In reality, finding an external facilitator for agile retrospectives is difficult due to cost or time constraints. Teams may also find they are the only people in their organisation that run retrospectives, making it impossible to find an experienced retrospective facilitator from anywhere else within their organisation.

Predicting the impact that a non-independent facilitator can have on the retrospective is difficult. The effects could be subtle, such as placing positive emphasis on a decision that they approve of. At other times, it could be obvious, for example if the facilitator skips discussion points they do not think are important, or spends more time on points they consider important. (I have witnessed all these behaviours.) Note that facilitators playing multiple roles may be completely unaware of their bias or how it affects a discussion during the retrospective.

A major reason for seeking an independent retrospective facilitator is to avoid a situation similar to the one I once experienced.

> I'd just joined a team that had been working together for a while. They held retrospectives every two weeks, organised and facilitated by their Project Manager. As the newest team member, I just observed how he ran the retrospective. I remember he pointed at one person at a time and asked for their input. He turned to write their input on to a flip chart before turning and pointing to the next person. If he didn't like the answer, he'd ask that person to think of another one. It took a good 15 minutes for him to work around the group and collect only one point from each person.

Combining the facilitator role with a leadership position is troublesome as it sends mixed signals to the group about what is acceptable. The facilitator role amplifies authority, and often reduces safety for participants and means that they are less willing to explore issues in depth. Some teams prefer a facilitator from within their ranks as they claim that it increases safety because everyone knows everyone else in the room. This increase in safety is only useful, however, if the facilitator can separate their own opinion from their role as a facilitator during the retrospective.

> In one organisation I worked with, two teams swapped a retrospective facilitator with each other so that everyone could focus on being a team-participant and didn't have to worry about who was going to facilitate.

3.2 Conflict of Interest

If you find yourself acting as a team member as well as a facilitator, you will inevitably need to deal with the conflict of interest that arises. The best thing to do is, during the 'Set the Stage' phase, declare your conflict of interest. Explain that you are facilitating and will sometimes have opinions that may interfere with your facilitation, however hard you try to keep them separate.

Encourage people to speak up if they feel that you are influencing rather than facilitating and be prepared to be pulled up for it. Be aware that just because you have given participants permission to pull you up does not guarantee that they will. To a certain extent, this depends on how your team or organisation views and respects positions of authority.

Use a visual cue to distinguish your different roles of 'facilitator' and 'participant'. One facilitator I saw wore a brightly coloured vest when they were acting as facilitator and quickly removed it when they wanted to express something as a participant. I have seen other teams use a large badge or a hat to help visualise the different roles.

If you cannot find any accessory to wear, try using different physical locations to 'step in' or 'step out' of role. At the very least, you should call out when you are expressing your opinion as a member or not. Another alternative is simply to agree with the other participants that the facilitator should focus on facilitation only and not contribute opinions to the retrospective at the risk of obscuring the whole picture.

3.3 Be Decisive

You've put together a plan detailing the exercises you would like to run and approximate timings. Remember that the role of the facilitator is to present a structure for people to hang their content from and start by explaining the exercises you're going to run and how long they should take. I have been part of many retrospectives where the facilitators asked the group what exercises they would like to run. Although I can relate to their desire to do the right thing by the group, the best thing for the group is to focus on the reflective process, not on the means of getting there.

If you suspect people may want something different, share your plan with the team beforehand and offer them a period for giving feedback so that you can incorporate it in the final plan. The retrospective is more fruitful when time is spent on the activities and then focusing participants back on the content. Encourage all feedback after the retrospective. If feedback is negative, you can explain the thinking behind the final plan and why you chose to focus on content rather than process.

3.4 Develop Your Facilitation Skills

Retrospectives take all the facilitation skills you can muster. They demand as much of a facilitator as any well run, effective group meeting. Don't make the mistake of treating the retrospective as a casually scheduled get-together with no agenda, like some that I have attended. Read up on the role of a facilitator, what behaviours make an effective facilitator, and what can make meetings more productive. The previous chapter gave a few basic pointers, and for more advice there are several books entirely devoted to facilitation skills and practices that I would recommend. I have listed some books to get you started in Appendix B.

See if you can take a facilitation course. Seek a course that allows you to practise and get immediate feedback from the course leader to help develop your self awareness. Learn what your facilitation strengths and weaknesses are and work on them.

Seek opportunities to facilitate other types of meetings and meet other facilitators. If there are other people in your organisation already running retrospectives, ask another facilitator to observe your facilitation during the retrospective, and then share their feedback with you after the retrospective. It's best not to receive feedback during the retrospective as you may find it throws off your concentration and your facilitation degrades.

Join the Retrospectives mailing list[1] and ask questions. Try to attend a Retrospective Facilitator's Gathering[2] as a way of connecting with other facilitators. This annual event, which alternates between North America and Europe, is a great opportunity to observe different styles and approaches to facilitation. It provides an almost retreat-like environment, which boosts safety and helps build relationships between facilitators to maximise learning and collaboration. I was awestruck by some of the other facilitators' skills and I learned a great deal from observing different facilitation styles and techniques in such a short timeframe. Importantly, I also learned how excellent facilitation can make a retrospective much more effective and meaningful.

3.5 Form Effective Actions

Change isn't expected to happen during the retrospective, so a common outcome for retrospectives is the group's agreement on what actions to take before the next retrospective. You can make an action more likely to happen by taking certain considerations into account.

Seek SMART Qualities

SMART is the acronym for: Specific, Measurable, Attainable, Relevant and Timely. Display these words some-

---

[1]http://groups.yahoo.com/group/retrospectives
[2]http://www.retrospectivefacilitatorgathering.org

where prominent and use them to steer participants into suggesting actions that match the criteria. For example, if someone says, 'We need to do more automated testing,' you might ask, 'What sort of automated testing? Performance testing? Unit testing? Acceptance testing? All of these?' or 'Can you quantify what you mean by "more"?'

Another common occurrence is for people to allocate actions to people not actually present at the retrospective. For example, you could counter something like, 'Our Operations people need to set up some monitoring,' with 'That's not something you can make happen. What is it that *you guys* can do?' A more acceptable action might be: 'Arrange a meeting with Operations to explain why we need monitoring and what the options are.'

Use the Plan of Action

A fellow retrospective facilitator, Bas Vodde created a technique called the Plan of Action[3]. The Plan of Action focuses people on the small incremental steps that can be made towards goals that are not easily solvable within a single iteration. He asks for participants to write down actions in the following form:

> **Long-term goal**: [Goal] **Now-action**: [Action]

Now-actions are what the team leaves the retrospective with; the long-term goal can be referred to throughout the

---

[3]http://www.scrumalliance.org/articles/61-plan-of-action

iteration to expand on further actions, or as input into the next retrospective.

Use the Six Action Shoes

The *Six Action Shoes*[DEBON] framework comes from the book of the same name by lateral thinker Edward De Bono. The framework proposes six 'shoes' and asks people:

a) What sort of shoe is needed for now? b) Put on those shoes and brainstorm actions.

The six shoes are described below:

- **Navy formal shoes** - The military is renowned for formal, routine behaviour. Routines help us to repeat tasks efficiently.
- **Grey sneakers** - Sneakers are quiet and don't attract attention. This shoe symbolises actions around exploration, investigation and collecting evidence or other information.
- **Brown brogues** - A classic shoe that symbolises pragmatic action; doing what can be done right now.
- **Orange gumboots** - Represents the fireman who deals with emergencies. Emergencies demand urgent, drastic action.
- **Pink slippers** - Representing comfort and cosiness, these symbolise compassionate actions involving human feelings and safety.
- **Purple riding boots** - Think of a general on horseback. Riding boots represent authority and so sym-

bolise 'Take charge' actions associated with particular roles.

This powerful thinking model can help people find the right way to approach a problem; by picking different shoes, they can brainstorm actions that fit each of these mental models.

Assign Action Owners

Even when actions conform to the SMART criteria, or are tied to a long-term goal, they are sometimes forgotten when everyone returns to their day job. To prevent this, make sure that every action is matched with one owner before leaving the retrospective. Try to avoid a situation where all actions are owned by one person, or by the people who usually take all the actions. Encourage everyone to take ownership of at least one action.

3.6 Spread the Retrospective Word

Look for ways you can encourage other people and teams to adopt retrospectives. Generally, there are one or two people in every group that would like to get better at facilitating. Consider taking them on as retrospective facilitator apprentices and show them what it could be like. Building a community of retrospective facilitators can prove an invaluable asset for both you and your organisation.

Teams can bring in other facilitators to keep energy levels and engagement fresh. Better still, rotate the facilitator role within the team and give feedback to each other after the retrospective to help improve everyone's facilitation skills. Facilitators tend to have a collection of favourite exercises, so other facilitators get to learn about these from each other, and everyone grows together. You can aim to develop more independent facilitators for each team.

Developing skills for effective retrospective facilitation will often help in other situations in your professional environment, agile-related or otherwise. You will learn to identify a poorly set-up meeting; understand why a meeting never reached its objectives, if any had been set at all, and you'll have more skills to enable teams to work in a more collaborative manner.

4 First-Time Facilitation Tips

Chances are you have not had any formal facilitation training unless you are a professional facilitator. Facilitation itself is a huge skill to develop, taking time and constant practice. Even though I have read, practised and facilitated many meetings, I still find myself with a lot of things to learn.

This section offers some advice for first-time facilitators, but I recommend using other formal training methods as these will assist you in other meetings. See Appendix B for recommended books to improve your facilitation skills.

In your role as a facilitator, you are responsible for the structure of the retrospective to help focus participants' attention strictly on the content. You want to make things easier for people by choosing the activities, the discussion formats and the pace of the meeting so they can focus on the subject, issues and analysis.

You will draw upon many tools and exercises to fulfil your responsibilities, which include keeping the meeting on track, handling conflicts, creating and maintaining safety of participants, getting closure on all issues raised and ensuring the correct information is captured. Remember that developing facilitation skills takes time and diligent practice.

4.1 Encourage Physical Presence

Establishing ground rules with participants at the start of the retrospective, or reiterating the existing rules helps set expectations about people and their participation. One basic ground rule should be to establish your expectations of participants and their physical presence.

As both a participant and a facilitator of retrospectives, I find it very distracting if others in the room are sitting with their laptops open or working on tablets or phones. Having other equipment switched on makes it easy for participants to slip into other topics, or to disengage completely from the retrospective. If participants are working on something else while at the retrospective, it sends the message to other participants in the room that it is okay to be distracted. If participants are distracted from the purpose of the meeting, it reduces the quality of the conversation. As a consequence of distracted participants you may find that you have to revisit topics already discussed, or that the team struggles to agree on suitable actions at the end of the retrospective because someone missed something earlier.

Establish with the group whether it is acceptable to bring laptops and electronic devices, and if so, how they should be used. One team I knew, for example, agreed for all electronic devices to be switched off except for phones linked to production support. This solution worked well. Whatever you decide as a group, you should encourage everyone to be physically and mentally engaged for the entire retrospective.

4.2 Seek Equal Participation

A common, shared picture is only possible if all participants give their input freely and share their view of the story. This is difficult if one or two people are allowed to dominate discussions. Part of your role as a facilitator is to use whatever techniques you can to ensure a balanced conversation occurs.

If only one person is speaking for much of the meeting, a technique you could use is to highlight this fact, and to invite others to give their opinion. It may be as simple as, 'I've noticed that Sally has had some time to contribute her view. I'm concerned that others may not feel the same, so, to ensure we have a balanced representation, I would like to hear some other viewpoints. I'd like to invite those who haven't yet spoken to contribute their thoughts.'

You might also consider breaking a large group into smaller groups for discussion, asking for a representative from each group to report back their findings. In this way a dominant person will be able to dominate only the small group rather than the conversations of the entire group.

Alternatively, consider asking participants to brain-storm input in silence before asking them to talk the group through what they've written. This gives an opportunity for every member to at least contribute.

If one person continues to dominate the group conversation, consider taking a break. If you anticipate a particular member dominating the conversations during a retrospective, approach them directly before the retrospective and explain your concerns to them. More often than not, the person doesn't realise how much they talk. Agree on a signal to indicate to the person that they are starting to talk too much and to help them to recognise when to pull back.

Also consider discussion formats that allocate chunks of time to each individual. The Circle of Questions comes from *Agile Retrospectives* [DERBY] and, as it suggests, requires participants to sit in a circle. Each person takes a turn to ask a question to their immediate left. The question may be anything, though it is best if it's focused on the retrospective topic. Be sure to prevent accusatory or offensive questions. The person to their left answers the question to their best of their ability and then, in turn, asks the person on their left a question. Their question may be the same question that they just answered in order to draw other responses. This continues until time runs out or the circle is completed at least twice. Ensure you complete the circle each time as skipping people sends the wrong message if some participants ask or answer more questions than others.

Another technique you might employ to prevent one person dominating is the Margolis Wheel [MARGO]. To set up a Margolis Wheel, arrange pairs of chairs (from four to six) in a circle as shown in the diagram below.

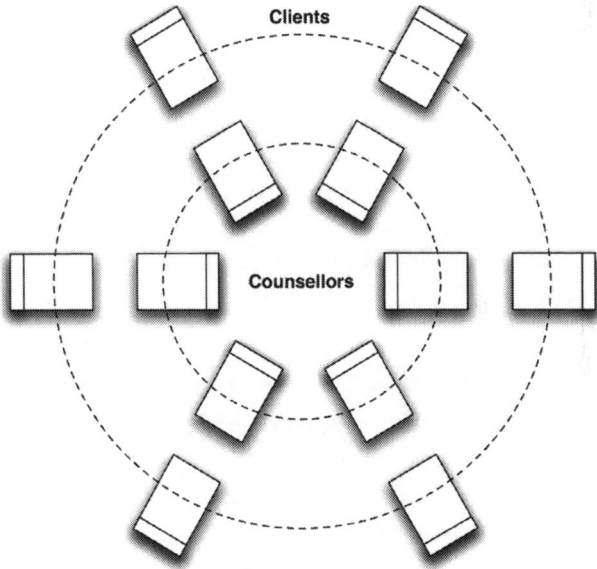

Six pairs of chairs arranged in the Margolis Wheel

Choose a topic and ask for everyone to sit in a chair. Those on the inner ring are considered Counsellors, those on the outer ring Clients. In this arrangement, Clients talk to Counsellors about their burning issue, with Counsellors offering advice, asking questions and helping the Clients think of potential solutions. In the context of a retrospective, this arrangement helps individuals see different points of views from different parts of the team. Use three minutes for each round of advice - roughly one minute for a Client to explain their problem, and two minutes for the Counsellor to talk through the impact and brainstorm potential solutions. After three minutes, the outer ring (Clients) move one seat to the right. The inner ring (Counsellors) remains seated. When the full circle is complete, the inner circle swaps places with the outer circle and the process repeated until changed. At the end of this exercise, work as part of the larger group to summarise any key findings or common themes and explore any action items suggested.

4.3 Avoid Doing All the Work Yourself

You may fall into the trap of some facilitators who like to control the writing, asking participants to call out items, which you then write up on a flip chart. This may be appropriate in other meetings, but during retrospectives you should seek as much participation from people as possible, including getting them to write down their thoughts.

When gathering data, or generating insights, hand out sticky notes and marker pens for people to write up their thoughts. Ask participants to place the sticky notes onto a wall or a flip chart sheet. You may notice sticky notes all related to a similar theme. Group them into a cluster. Instead of you walking through items, invite members to walk through clusters. Your role can then focus on highlighting clusters that are accidentally skipped.

By inviting more participation you are really trying to facilitate ownership of the meeting by the team, and hopefully encourage more ownership of the actions by the end of the retrospective.

4.4 Confirm Your Understanding

When you write up actions of what you hear, read it back to the group to confirm that you have interpreted it correctly. It is frustrating for participants if a written up message does not convey what they intended. If the group is moving too fast, ask everyone to wait until you have captured something, and check that what you have captured reflects the discussion before moving on.

Alternatively, you may ask the group to capture some of the information, but be sure to confirm with the wider group that the captured statements reflect the conversation. Confirming the captured statements increases the chance for the team to recognise and own the output at the end of a retrospective. When writing or reading back, I recommend using the exact words that people used. Avoid paraphrasing as people interpret this as not being listened to.

4.5 Rephrase Blaming Statements

If things get heated during a retrospective, people tend to forget the spirit of the Prime Directive and start talking about participants. You should be prepared to jump in quickly to protect the safety of the retrospective atmosphere, where you want people to talk openly about issues, and prevent blame.

Encourage the use of 'I-language' from participants, and help people to rephrase their statements if given in a blaming way. I-language focuses people on their own observations and experiences, helping to move away from labelling that may be interpreted as blame.

For example, if someone says, 'Bob doesn't care about the build,' point out that this is a judging statement and ask them to rephrase the sentence from their own point of view, using I-language. An improvement to the previous statement might be: 'I feel upset that Bob broke the build four times yesterday.'

It takes time to develop good listening skills. It helps to look for distinct sections in what people say. Separate facts from feelings and feelings from judgements; look for strategies to deal with them separately. Allow people to first state facts, and confirm whether others recognise what has been said. Allow people to talk about their feelings and work to acknowledge them. Prevent people from placing judgements on others as this works to destroy the safety that is important in open discussions during a retrospective.

4.6 Keep the Focus on the Current Phase

One of the key responsibilities of the facilitator is ensuring that everyone progresses through the five phases of the retrospective at the same pace. You may feel that some people are itching to get to action items or to discuss the impact of the data that others are writing, but jumping around within the phases will cause confusion and potentially prevent agreement on final actions.

If team members want to talk about actions or the impact of something, acknowledge this and explain that you will get there shortly. Try something like, 'I hear you are keen to decide on what to do, but in this exercise we are exploring what happened. We will get around to discussing what to do afterwards, but it's important we first share a common understanding of the situation at hand.'

4.7 Use a Visual Agenda

Sometimes team members bring up issues that, though important, may not be relevant to the purpose of the retrospective. Instead of focusing on events, issues and ways to improve, they might want to focus on solving a problem they see as pressing, such as the way to design a particular feature, or brainstorming how they might meet security requirements. These topics may be important, but often best dealt with in a meeting specific to that purpose.

One technique I often use is to ensure that the purpose

of the retrospective is written up on a flip chart and displayed. I then use this to draw attention to topics that are not necessarily relevant. Acknowledge the topic the person is referring to, but ask if it meets the aim of the retrospective meeting, or if a different meeting with different participants is more appropriate.

Another common facilitation technique is to use a Parking Lot, or a flip chart, to acknowledge topics but to park discussion until the end of the meeting, when you should revisit them and decide what to do. Write up a placeholder for the topic being discussed as this helps people feel their concerns have been acknowledged and make sure you close it at the end. A perfectly acceptable solution may be to organise a different meeting with the sole purpose of addressing that topic.

Make sure you address all the parking lot issues at the end of the retrospective. Addressing them may be as simple as asking people if the issue needs addressing right now, or if a different group of people needs to be involved to address the issue. Do not, under any circumstance, ignore parking lot issues as participants feel that their issue has not been addressed and if you want to try to park an issue in a future retrospective, they will resist.

4.8 Use a Wide Variety of Questions

Questions are a powerful tool in the facilitator's kit. The right questions at the right time can help guide teams into deeper insights of topics. They help to clarify important information and can be used to seek consensus from the greater group. Consider combining the different question styles listed below during retrospectives:

- **Open Ended** - Questions that cannot easily be answered with a 'yes' or 'no'; these help draw further explanations out into the open. These questions often start with 'How?', 'What?' or 'Why?'
- **Probing** - Much like open-ended questions, probing questions seek a greater response looking for much more detail. Probing questions might start with words like, 'Describe', 'Tell' or 'Explain'.
- **Redirecting** - These questions reflect a statement back at the group; useful for ensuring equal participation amongst members. For example, 'What do the rest of you think of...?' or 'Can others express their opinion of...?'
- **Feedback and Clarification** - These questions help to reinforce the current thread of talk and are useful before capturing the output on a flip chart. These might begin with, 'Did I hear you correctly, and you just said...?' or 'Can someone offer a summary of our position?'
- **Close Ended** - These are useful for bringing closure to topics, and confirming the group's thoughts after a team has had a longer discussion. 'Does everyone better understand the background to...?' or 'Is everyone happy with this action?' or 'Should we move on to the next topic?'

Be careful to use questions in the right circumstance. For example, drawing upon too many close-ended questions early in a retrospective may limit the amount of discussion and lead to frustrated participants. Likewise, using too many open-ended questions at the end of a retrospective may prevent appropriate closure, also leading to frustrated participants. Experiment with your questioning style and read more about which questions to use when in other books on facilitation such as the *Facilitator's Guide to Participatory Decision-Making* [KANER]

4.9 Observe Body Language

In your role as a facilitator you will be occupied listening to what people say. In addition, you should watch for the non-verbal cues that people send, as these are as meaningful as the verbal. Learn to look for patterns and their potential meaning, making mental notes and deciding what to do with them.

For example, someone sitting upright and forward might start to open their mouth, and then suddenly sit back because someone else has decided to have their say. This pattern is typical of someone who wanted to contribute but felt the opportunity had passed. As a facilitator, you should notice the pattern and re-create an opportunity for them to speak up: 'Mary, were you going to add something to the discussion?' may encourage the person to say what they originally intended.

If several people are sitting back in their chairs and

staring out of the window, it might mean that the group is not as engaged as it could be. You might reflect this back at the group as a talking point, 'I notice that participation is low during the retrospective and people appear to be distracted. Is there something going on and should we continue the retrospective?' Group lethargy may be caused by something as simple as people still digesting after lunch, but raising it as a concern could uncover a deeper issue that wasn't being raised verbally.

> TIP: To avoid a dip in energy levels due to digestion, avoid scheduling retrospectives after lunch. Alternatively, run an activity that gets people on their feet to wake them up. Avoid rooms that are too warm as that will also send people off to sleep.

4.10 Observe Yourself

The facilitator's energy has a direct impact on the retrospective. It took me a while to appreciate this, but you may have already noticed it in the retrospectives you facilitate. If you act nervous, cross your arms, or come across as hesitant, participants often reflect this back with less open conversations, or the retrospective tends to have a more tense atmosphere.

Lack of energy in a facilitator directly translates into a flat-feeling retrospective with an equal lack of energy. Ensure your full attention and energy is present to serve the group, and that you show visible signs of engage-ment. Be wary of being too energetic and boisterous as an introverted group might find it unpleasant and sit uncomfortably through your retrospective.

Even if you are nervous, try to appear as calm as you possibly can when facilitating. It helps to take long, deep breaths. Keep the conversation as open as possible, setting an example by keeping your arms at your side, not crossed. Avoid putting hands in pockets, leaning or sitting. If it helps, take hold of a pen that you plan on writing with, or an index card with the schedule of the retrospective. These inconspicuous tools can be supportive props and prevent other people noticing your nerves.

Make eye contact with participants, look into their faces, not just the face of one or two, or even worse their feet. Remember to smile and to stand straight as your posture and tone convey confidence in the retrospective you have prepared.

5 Distributed Retrospectives

5.1 Distributed Challenges

Agile methodologies encourage as much face-to-face communication as possible. Getting the client and the development team to meet in the same place (co-locating) is almost assumed as a starting point for agile teams. In reality, co-locating presents challenges due to constraints such as project size; diversity and availability of skills, and the difference in labour costs. As with any activity involving people, communication will always be richer when everyone is co-located.

For a retrospective to have the greatest impact, it is recommended to run it with all the distributed team members in the same place. Distributed retrospectives can be frustrating for participants and often take much longer than an equivalent co-located one. Difficulties with technology and misunderstandings arising have a direct impact on the quality of the output; I cannot emphasise enough the value of bringing people physically together as much as possible.

In distributed meetings, conversations flow less fluidly. Interruptions and interjections become more difficult to deal with as time-lag causes conversations to overlap. Misunderstandings are more likely to occur when people cannot use physical cues of body language or facial expressions. An offhand comment that was meant ironically can be interpreted as offensive. Low-quality audio affects everyone in every location, not just remote participants. Low-quality audio means that people have to repeat themselves and it is more demanding for listeners at the other end.

Distributed retrospectives present additional challenges, but you can make them more effective with the right preparation and compensating practices. Even with these practices, the quality of the output will not match one where everyone is together in the same place.

Distributed retrospectives come in a variety of forms and each has side effects that you will need to consider.

Small Group of Remote Participants

This situation arises when there is a large group of participants in one location and one person, or a few people are in a remote location. I have seen this in organisations where people are allowed to work remotely, or where the project requires a particular specialism, which is provided by someone who can't always be physically present. The facilitator often sits in the same room as the larger group, with the remote participants dialling in via a phone line or video line.

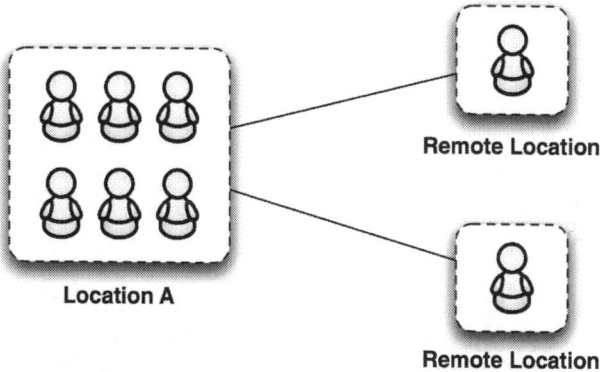

Example of a small group of remote participants

Common problems that arise with this situation is that the discussions of the larger group dominate the retrospective time and remote participants do not participate as actively as those present in the room.

Bad phone lines or connections can make it difficult for remote participants to be heard, and it is easier for the group to talk over someone because they are not visible. In addition, remote participants can feel that they are interrupting, or that it is harder to share their side of the story, with the result that they simply remain quiet.

Groups of Equal Size in Different Locations

This type of retrospective is most common with offshore development, or a development model that involves around-the-clock shifts. Participants are usually split fairly evenly across locations and the retrospective brings them together via electronic means. A facilitator often sits with one of the groups and the other group dials in.

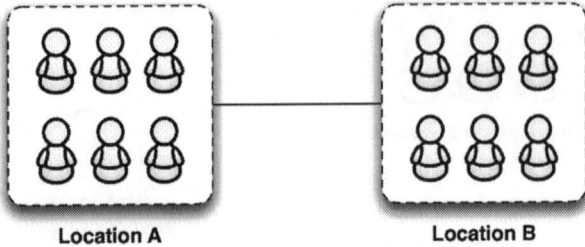

Location A   **Location B**

Example of a group equally distributed

The most common problem that arises with this type are the break-out conversations that happen between each group. Remote facilitation is difficult and allowing people to flow into discussion and then reining it back in against deadlines proves difficult.

Wholly Distributed Participants

This type of retrospective has participants scattered across many locations, and often many time zones. Almost every participant is dialling in via a phone line, with little face-to-face visibility of the entire group. These type of retrospectives are the most difficult to run effectively.

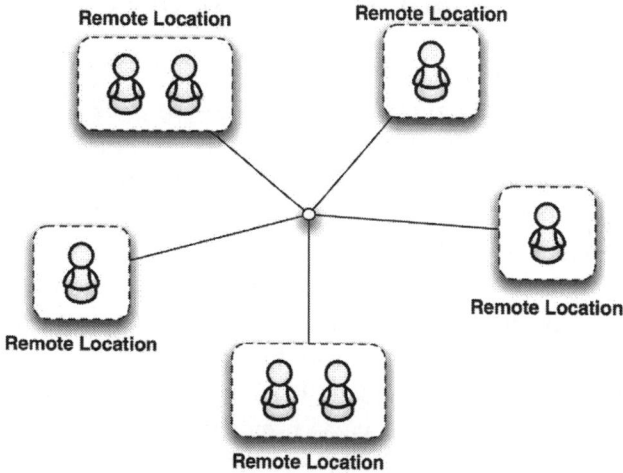

Example of a group completed distributed

Co-ordinating activities and focusing on a single story becomes troublesome as there are delays and drop-outs in communication. A participant may go offline and conversations will still be flowing without the realisation that someone who might have something to add to the perspective is no longer there.

If everyone is calling in, it is sometimes more difficult to understand the flow, depending on where they are calling from. At one distributed retrospective I was in, for example, a participant was calling from the airport, so all that other participants could hear was the noise of the terminal with flights being announced.

5.2 Make the Most of It

Fortunately, many teams obliged to work in a distributed way have found a number of approaches that help make distributed retrospectives more effective. These approaches can never replace the experience of a single, fully co-located retrospective but with a little trial and error, may be enough for what your team needs.

With any of these practices, I'd encourage you to see what best fits your environment. Practices that work well for one team often fail to fit the needs and culture of another team. In an agile fashion, trial these approaches and then inspect and adapt accordingly.

5.3 Focus First on Building Relationships

One of the most important outcomes of a retrospective is ensuring that everyone's point of view is heard in a group. Where there is low trust between people, issues are often not raised, and even when they are, rarely in great detail. Doing this in a distributed manner, where there are faceless voices becomes even more difficult.

Focus on activities that work to build relationships and connections between team members. Consider making the first activity one where members introduce themselves, share their personal interests and help members in different locations to connect. A simple example is getting people to prepare 'Two Truths and a Lie' - where others have to guess which statement someone shares is untrue. Find an ice-breaker exercise that is relevant to the topic or situation as some people regard a random activity as a waste of time and so it can create a bad impression of what is to follow.

Invest in the first retrospective most of all and bring participants face-to-face. Organise a social event before or after the first retrospective to create and strengthen the relationships between members. These social bonds help to enrich the next distributed retrospective you run. It really helps for people to be able to picture the face that belongs to the disembodied voice coming out of a telephone.

5.4 Use Video Cameras at All Ends

Higher internet bandwidth and better infrastructure in many parts of the world mean that distributed teams often have more than just a telephone as an option when holding a retrospective. Aim for the highest quality video equipment that your organisation can afford and ensure that video is shared equally among participants. Consider alternative mechanisms as the level of distribution goes up.

> I ran a retrospective that used Microsoft Roundtable, now called Polycom CX5000HD[1] for a team that had participants dialling in from four locations. It works by having a fully 360-degree panoramic view, also showing separate

---

[1]http://www.polycom.com/products/voice/conferencing_solutions/microsoft_optimized_conferencing/cx5000.html

windows for all participants dialling in via their home web cameras. Its main window adjusts to automatically highlight who is currently speaking, so it feels more like remote participants are physically there.

5.5 People Tokens in Remote Locations

One team I know ran a distributed retrospective with three people dialling in from various remote locations to the rest of the group. The team allowed three extra chairs in the meeting room, and on each chair was a large cuddly toy with a life-sized headshot photo attached to represent each of the people dialling in.

One team member, physically present in the retrospective, enthused about the interesting effect it had on the retrospective: 'It really felt like the three team members were present in the room. I think we were quicker to stop and listen to them when they spoke over the phone, as we imagined them physically being in the room.'

While I'm not sure it's for everyone, I can imagine it might work for some. Give it a go.

5.6 Prevent Remote People 'Going Dark'

A frequent occurrence in distributed retrospectives, particularly when there is one large group and a handful of remote participants, is what I call, 'Going Dark'. The group that is physically present tend to run away with the discussion and comes to a decision without remembering to invite input from remote participants. It's hard to know whether the decision is the right one without everyone's input, especially without any visual feedback from remote participants.

One thing that good facilitators do during distributed retrospectives is to regularly poll everyone for their opinion. The facilitator really emphasises the opinion of the remote participants to ensure that there is a fair amount of input.

This can seem odd at first, but it does help remote people feel more positive about the retrospective and contribute more to the meeting.

5.7 Faces for Everyone

Distributed teams that work together rarely get to physically meet. If none of the previous approaches to distributed meetings are feasible, it's good to at least make sure that everyone knows what everyone else looks like at the start. Good preparation for a distributed retrospective may mean collecting recent photos of all participants and distributing the list of names and photos via a wiki or email.

5.8 Use Remote Facilitators

Some teams run distributed retrospectives with facilitators in all locations. The facilitators must do more work to prepare for the retrospective, agreeing on what the agenda will be, who will facilitate which parts, and the mechanism to ensure good, constant communication between the different groups.

The result is often higher-quality communication and a retrospective where all participants have an equal opportunity to contribute and be heard. The facilitators work with each other to ensure that voices on either side are heard, and ensure that all inputs are captured and represented on the other side.

5.9 Collect Input Before the Meeting

Some teams collect input before the meeting and use the retrospective to drive discussion around the impact and the actions that need to happen. Facilitators should aim to get participants to brainstorm only facts or events, rather than describing impact and suggested actions. Gathering too much data prior to the meeting can lead to misunderstandings and so it is preferable to have as much transparency as possible by having relevant conversations synchronously. This depends, of course, on the level of trust between the team members.

Sometimes the time gained by getting everyone to give their input is lost in ensuring that everyone understands what all the input was and how it's related. Making sure that everyone has the same view of the data is important for progressing the retrospective to the next phases.

5.10 Use Online Tools to Share

Retrospectives generate a lot of information. Capturing it and ensuring that everyone can see it is easy when all participants are physically present. When participants are facing different ways or are in different locations makes this trickier. There are different mechanisms to share the information as it's happening. Some of these include:

- Real-time document-collaboration tools, such as Sync.in[2] and Google Docs[3] where multiple people can edit the same document in real-time and see various contributions. This is great as you can see people capturing information in real-time. Names and highlighting can help too if you need to run Dot Voting[4]
- Mindmeister[5] is a real-time mind-map tool for collaboration. Consider using branches to group stickies into groups or to represent the different arms of 'Went Well', 'Less Well' and 'Puzzles'.
- Shared online boards, such as Lino it[6], edistorm[7], Bubbl.us[8], and Wallwisher[9].
- IdeaBoardz[10] is an online tool specifically for distributed retrospectives.
- Instant Messaging Tools are useful for capturing input in a single location.

5.11 Agree on a Signalling System

Even with high-quality video conferencing or telephone systems, one of the greatest challenges of the distributed

---

[2]http://sync.in/
[3]https://docs.google.com
[4]http://en.wikipedia.org/wiki/Dotmocracy
[5]http://www.mindmeister.com
[6]http://www.linoit.com
[7]http://www.edistorm.com
[8]https://bubbl.us/
[9]http://www.wallwisher.com/
[10]http://www.ideaboardz.com

retrospective is to ensure that the conversation flows. One side often dominates a conversation and interruptions and time-lags in remote communication mean it's hard for the other side to interject easily without interrupting the flow of the discussion. This can be frustrating for both parties as it doesn't feel natural.

Agree on a mechanism for participants to 'signal' when they want to speak to the other party. In one distributed retrospective with a single remote participant, we decided to use Skype[11] at both ends. We agreed to use the chat feature, not for conversation, but solely for the remote participant to indicate when they wanted to add something to the conversation. The facilitator took note and redirected the conversation to the remote participant at a suitable moment, helping the conversation to flow more naturally.

5.12 Invest in a 'Technographer'

Facilitating, done well, takes time and energy. Paying attention to technical environments such as phone lines dropping, or responding to electronic media problems prevents the facilitator from focusing on the conversation.

Some teams elect or invite a 'technographer' to their session whose role is to make sure that all communication devices work properly. The technographer monitors all the devices like a hawk, trying to fix something as soon as it comes up.

---

[11]http://www.skype.com

A true technographer will act as a scribe, capturing and distributing information during the session by transcription or by driving the live, electronic media that's being used. This means that the participants can focus on their discussion and the facilitator can focus on making the retrospective itself effective.

5.13 Run Remote Working Groups

A common technique in larger retrospectives is to break them up into smaller groups to work on a set of action items, and then to discuss these with the wider audience. It allows for more conversation threads at the risk of getting different conclusions. Some distributed teams choose this approach when running an activity such as brainstorming across different locations; summarising it and then having a representative from each location share the outcome with the other group.

5.14 Remote Proxies as Representatives

In a group where most people are in one location and a few participants are working remotely, you could use a remote proxy. With this technique, one person in the meeting room stays in direct contact with the remote participants via Instant Messenger (IM). The remote participants use IM to indicate that they want to speak and their 'proxy' relays this to the facilitator or the group. The facilitator then opens up the conversation for the remote participant to present their point of view over the phone.

Having a proxy helps remote participants feel just as valued as people physically present. This mechanism allows participants to indicate that they would like to make a contribution without talking over someone and avoids the confusion that ensues when you try to do this over the phone, where there can be noise and delay.

If a phone line is bad, you may opt to relay all remote conversation through a proxy. I would discourage adopting this as common practice, however, as I think it is better for people to connect with the remote participant by hearing their voice, instead of the proxy's.

5.15 Simple Tips for Remote Communication

Finally, here are some simple rules to help make distributed retrospectives more effective.

- Go for the highest-quality headphones and headsets. It's really important to hear people as clearly as possible.
- Prefer a wired internet connection over wi-fi. Prefer wi-fi over roaming internet. Higher bandwidths are better for avoiding time-lag and interrupted conversational flow.
- Prefer a wired telephone line over a mobile telephone as the line is more stable.

- People dialling in should do so from a quiet room, preferably away from anyone else. Background noise makes it more difficult to understand participants. If the caller can't find a quiet place, agree for them to mute while they are listening in order to minimise background noise.
- Ensure all computers are plugged into the mains. There's nothing worse than finding that someone has gone offline because their laptop battery was flat.
- Remote participants should book their quiet room for the entire duration of the meeting to prevent having to disconnect and reconnect in search of another quiet space.

5.16 Be Aware of Cultural Dimensions

Distribution often presents the challenge of different cultures working together. Geert Hofstede is well known for his studies describing different cultural dimensions [HOFST] and the impact they have on working relationships. These are difficult to overcome in person, and need to be taken into account when working remotely. He identified the following cultural dimensions for national cultures:

- **Power Distance Index (PDI)** - The extent to which the less powerful members of organisations and institutions accept and expect that power is distributed unequally. People participating in retrospectives from a culture with a lower PDI are more likely to challenge or question what someone has said, regardless of the other's role. People from a culture with a higher PDI are more likely to not mention anything.

- **Individualism versus Collectivism** - The degree to which individuals are integrated into groups. People from cultures with high degree of individualism may constantly discuss items from their own point of view rather than from the whole teams'.

- **Uncertainty Avoidance Index** - A society's tolerance for uncertainty and ambiguity. Retrospective participants from a culture of low uncertainty avoidance are more likely to give the impact of random events lower priority. This may generate more conflict on the relative importance of events, and also, deciding what to do.

- **Masculinity versus Femininity** - The distribution of emotional roles between the genders. Participants from cultures with different focuses may focus on different topics as part of a retrospective. According to Hofstede, masculine attributes include competitiveness, assertiveness and ambition, which contrast with typically feminine priorities, such as relationships and quality of life. Bringing participants together from cultures where these focuses are different may be frustrating to participants.

- **Long-Term Orientation versus Short-Term Orientation** - How much a society prioritises the long-term future over the short term. Participants from a culture of short-term orientation tend to look for immediate actions and quick fixes that may be easier to do, but may not help in the long run.
- **Indulgence versus Restraint** - What cultural norms exist that encourage or discourage immediate fulfilment of desires.

The facilitator should expect a larger distribution of cultural dimensions when running the retrospective distributively. During discussions, facilitators must anticipate areas of potential conflict due to different culture norms and be prepared to mediate behaviours caused by these differences. For example, if the facilitator is working with a team from a lower PDI culture, and remotely with a team from a high PDI culture, they should encourage the remote team to speak their voice first and actively seek to remove the perception of any hierarchy between participants.

5.17 Distributed Retrospectives Are Always Harder

I feel that retrospectives where all participants are in the same physical location will always be more effective than when some participants are located elsewhere. However, I know that not all teams are lucky enough to avoid distribution. Hopefully all of these tips will help teams obliged to work distributively to run a more effective retrospective.

6 Other Flavours of Retrospectives

The agile manifesto is now more than ten years old and the practice of retrospectives is older still. With so many teams using the retrospective practice, it is understandable that teams want to try new variants. This chapter describes variations that you might find immediately useful, or that may inspire you to adapt the retrospective practice in a completely new manner.

6.1 Futurespectives

As the name suggests, retrospectives focus on looking back in order to improve the future. Futurespectives, inspired by one of the Innovation Games[1], 'Remember the Future', and first introduced to me by Tim MacKinnon, work by thinking about the future and seeking insights and actions to secure a future vision. These are great exercises to run just as a new initiative is kicking off. Several variants now exist, but here's how I would typically run one. Expect it to last about an hour.

1. **Set the Stage** by presenting the future - Tell the audience, 'Imagine we just stepped into a time machine and teleported to the time just after the completion of your project. It's been so successful, the project sponsors have set aside this time to do a project

---

[1]http://innovationgames.com/

retrospective. We are going to explore during this session the ups, downs, and key activities that made this project successful.'

At this point you will unveil the timeline from now to the end of the project, with some visual indicator of where the team are (at the end of the timeline). Explain the timeline, 'The project had many successful events and I'd like you to describe each event on a separate sticky note in green. There may have been some things that didn't go well, for which I'd like a separate sticky note in red. However, you always overcame these difficulties and these events should be followed by what successful actions you took to overcome that difficulty on a green sticky note.'

1. **Gather Data** - Leave people to brainstorm events and place the events on the timeline. Encourage people to start with positive green items first and ensure red items are counteracted with green events that overcame each problem. Introduce the 'Jacuzzi Card' - ask people to think of a crazy idea to influence their project (eg. office on an aeroplane). Pick several roles and ask representatives to walk the group through the project, telling a story about some of the items on the timeline as they occurred.

2. **Generate Insights** - With a timeline providing data, mine the information using other retrospective activities such as 'Well, Less Well, Puzzles' or 'Voting on Top Items to Discuss'.

3. **Decide What to Do** - At this point, drive people back to the present and ask people, 'With a view of the future, what actions will you take away to help you deliver a successful project according to this future vision.'

4. **Close the Retrospective** - Recap what you just did and confirm those actions. Help people feel like they have an influence over the future and the ability to complete all the actions they set out to do. Thank participants for their contributions and close the futurespective.

Material and Preparation:

You will need a lot of space for this exercise, so find a room with a large wall where you can display several flip charts together, or find a whiteboard wall to use. Place some 'marker events' at the top of the timeline to provide examples and invite the group to add more marker events (eg. Company Conference, Christmas, Release Date). Use a different coloured sticky note (eg. yellow) for marker events to avoid confusion with other input you collect.

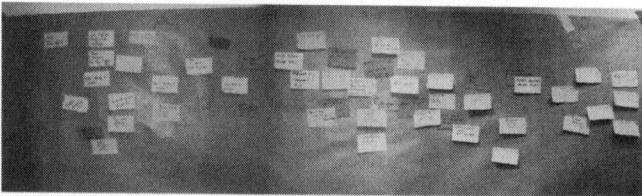

Futurespective Timeline

6.2 Continuous Retrospectives

The idea behind Continuous Retrospectives is inspired by the retrospective practice. I do not see Continuous Retrospectives fulfilling the same needs as a retrospective because some of the key elements, such as the shared story and conversations, tend to be missing. However, the Continuous Retrospective, sometimes called a Continuous Feedback Board, proves a popular and effective mechanism for improvements within a certain context, and therefore an important tool to add to your kit.

A number of agile events use Continuous Retrospectives to actively gather and immediately act on any feedback. At XP2009, a five-day conference, the organisers established a wall with sticky notes, markers and some clearly marked columns. They used this input to change the conference and act on any feedback provided the day before. For conferences, a Continuous Retrospective wall is best placed towards the entrance or exit or somewhere that people tend to gather, such as where refreshments are served. These are places where people will be inclined to naturally wander over to look at what people have put up, often stopping to put up an item themselves.

Conference organisers find this format works well to enable them to respond and improve a conference over its timespan, but Continuous Retrospectives do have their drawbacks. Firstly, the conversation can be one-way, with attendees putting up whatever they like without any motivation to help or implement improvements. Secondly, some of the feedback may include actions that are not feasible (eg. move the venue to a different location!) or that are unlikely to be achieved until after the period, whilst other pieces of data contradict each other, leading to confusion about what can possibly be done (eg. room too hot versus room too cold).

Some teams establish a Continuous Retrospective wall to gather retrospective data. Members are encouraged to put up sticky notes with their input on the wall. Minor items that other team members feel they can address are dealt with immediately and taken down. A significant number of notes left on the wall after a pre-determined period then triggers a normal retrospective with the notes providing the input for the retrospective.

6.3 Very Big Retrospectives

As a group gets larger, running retrospectives becomes more of a challenge. Generally speaking, I would consider a retrospective with 20 or more participants to be 'very big'. In a very big retrospective, it's easier for an individual to lose engagement and hide in the crowd; multiple conversations are more likely to break out concurrently, making it difficult for participants to build a shared story. It is often more difficult to reach a consensus with so many people wanting to do different things.

Here are tips to help you run very big retrospectives more effectively.

- **Allow more time** - Firstly expect to cover the same

activities and level of discussion in a longer time. Moving a larger group takes more time. Reconvening after break-out discussions will take longer and you need to allow for this in your schedule.

- **Use multiple facilitators** - When working with a large group, it's useful to have someone co-facilitate so that you can take turns supporting each other. One person focuses on the current conversation, while the other distributes materials, puts up flip charts, or clarifies what the current activity is for sub groups. Make sure you meet up before the retrospective so that neither of you are surprised by the order of the activities and to help each other to prepare.

- **Use break-out groups** - Collecting a large group's input in one go will result in an information overload. It's particularly boring if one person is reading out everyone's inputs as well. Make use of working groups and ensure each group is diverse enough to prevent data being skewed unintentionally. Ask people to brainstorm data in their groups. Ask someone to summarise the discussions for the rest of the group. Really focus on keeping participants engaged by getting working groups to present what they have to the wider audience. Resist the temptation to read out a group's input yourself.

- **Consider mixing up the groups** - If you sense individual groups suffering from too much homogeneity or groupthink and feel this is affecting their output, run an activity that distributes people randomly. For example, put numbered strips of paper into a hat or bag, and ask people to pull out a numbered strip. Ask people to reassemble into new groups based on the number written on the paper strip.

- **Lean on group work** - Doing deep dives into discussions as a whole group will be a frustrating experience as it tends to engage only those people who are comfortable talking in front of a large crowd. This may lead to a very skewed picture and outcome. Instead, after collecting initial data, see if you can identify themes and then allocate a different theme to each working group to focus on a retrospective activity to generate insights. Ask each group to summarise their findings and present the summary of their theme to the group.

- **Prioritise work** - Use techniques like dot voting once you have done as much grouping into themes as possible. This will give you a sense of which topics are the most urgent for discussion. If you think there may be an imbalance (eg. there are more developers than UX people), try to address it by allocating extra votes or restricting the number of votes. Explain why you're doing this and why a balanced prioritisation process is important.

- **Self-organise owners for actions** - When groups have generated actions, avoid the slow, painful process of asking people who will own what. A useful technique I have seen is to get group members to write the actions down on large index cards and then pin these up side by side, across a wall or large whiteboard. Ask the group to walk along the wall and if they feel comfortable owning an action, ask them to mark their name beneath that action (people can volunteer to own more than one!) or, alternatively, ask people to stand beneath or next to the action that they would like to own. It soon becomes apparent which actions have no owners and you can then facilitate a discussion around potential owners for those.

- **Use the fishbowl discussion** - I describe the fishbowl in a later section and this tends to be a good alternative for having a discussion deep dive where everyone has the opportunity to get involved.

6.4 Very Small Retrospectives

Just as very big retrospectives have their own character, very small retrospectives (1-4 people) are different again. Retrospectives for one person are particularly special, so I'll discuss those separately.

Personal Retrospectives

Retrospective facilitator Ainsley Nies is known for her work on the Personal Retrospective format. I recommend her latest presentation, which is available online[2].

---

[2]http://www.infoq.com/presentations/Personal-Retrospectives

I try to do a personal retrospective every year. I find the ritual helps me to remember my successes and to set my goals for the year ahead. A key element, and what I find the biggest hurdle, is explicitly setting aside time and space to the personal retrospective. It is easy to make excuses and let time slip, but you really can benefit from booking a good block of time for yourself to focus on retrospecting. Unlike agile retrospectives, which require co-ordinating with others to find a suitable time, personal retrospectives can and should take place over several periods in close succession. Looking at the same data over several different periods close together (a number of hours on several consecutive days, for example) often brings new insights.

Find a quiet, private place away from distractions, such as computers, radio or TV. If you like to have music on in the background, opt for something soft or acoustic that won't interfere with your thoughts.

I still like to use sticky notes for brainstorming on my own, but a notepad and pen works just as well. I use the same activities I would use for a large retrospective, with the main difference being that I don't need a large wall or white board. I choose a table or floor space to lay out stickies, or a large piece of paper to draw the timeline.

Consider recording your notes in an easy-to-use format that you can easily refer to. You may find a large sketchpad works well, or mind-mapping tools. It's important you find a tool you feel comfortable with, but that does not distract from the reflective process.

The process for me still follows the five stages, making

sure I step through gathering data before generating insights. Rather than invent questions to stimulate insights, I try to prepare these beforehand and then when I run the personal retrospective, pretend a facilitator is asking me the questions and I fully engage on trying to focus on the answers. It sounds strange, but I find it helpful to picture a facilitator. I know some colleagues who ask their coach or mentor to act as the facilitator and help them step through this process. I then wrap up by thinking about the future and come up with actions, tending to favour the Plan of Action, because I tend to have more long-term goals with immediate actions than short-term ones.

Small Group Retrospectives

The dynamics of a small-group retrospective (2-4 people) are very different from those of a larger group. The conversations are more intimate as there are fewer participants and there is more likely to be a break in the conversation. You are more likely to have a conflict of interest as it is even harder to justify an independent facilitator for a small group than it is for a large one. Nevertheless, you should try to get a facilitator if you can. Offer to do an exchange with someone in another team: if they facilitate for your team, you can do the same for them in return.

If you anticipate tense issues cropping up, all the more reason to make the Prime Directive visible and remembered throughout the retrospective. Make sure safety is high, with a separate room, and attempt to have everyone contribute equally. If conversation gets heated between two key members, work to diffuse the tension. Try getting everyone to contribute to a single wall, and if there are key issues between specific individuals, you may want to consider finding a mediator who could run a separate workshop on relationship-building.

To get equal contribution from members, use a large wall that everyone can access and get everyone to put their data and insights up there. Try asking someone to tell the story of an event that was put up by someone else so that they can better appreciate what others may be seeing. The Circle of Questions exercise from Agile Retrospectives [DERBY] proves really powerful in small groups, because it relies on participants rather than the facilitator to pose questions, and each builds on the energy of the previous question.

Small group retrospectives tend to take less time as fewer participants are building the shared picture. Small groups also tend to have closer working relationships already and this accelerates the retrospective and quickly results in focused actions for people to take away.

6.5 Appreciative Inquiry Retrospectives

What happens when everything is running well? What value do retrospectives have when customers are happy with what your team delivers and the process appears to be running well? You may choose to run less frequent retrospectives or you may want to consider **Appreciative**

Inquiry (AI) retrospectives.

It's easy for teams to focus more on 'What went less well?' instead of celebrating and recognising 'What went well.' Assuming that there are problems that need to be addressed often sets a negative tone, which in turn leads to a sombre mood at the end of a retrospective. AI retrospectives aim to shift this emphasis by focusing on recognising and building upon the team's strengths and successes. The actions from an AI retrospective should build upon the team's positive aspects, leading to more energy and momentum to go forward.

> **What is Appreciative Inquiry?** The AI movement has a long history researching the impact of focusing on the positive and aligns well with the Positive Psychology movement. You can read more about the AI movement in David L. Cooperrider and Diana Whitney's paper, *A Positive Revolution in Change: Appreciative Inquiry* [COOPE].

The AI movement follows a cycle that typically involves four elements:

1. **Discover** - Identifying the current strengths of an organisation, team or situation and positive elements that currently work well.
2. **Dream** - Imagining processes or a future of potentially working even better.
3. **Design** - Exploring what needs to be done or who needs to be involved to make the dream a reality.

4. **Deliver** - Implementing the design as envisaged.

Applying these four elements to a retrospective affects what questions you ask as well as how you might shape the discussion. There is no single way to run an AI retrospective as the focus is more on the conversation, but here is an example of how you might prepare and run an AI retrospective.

1. **Set the stage** - Welcome everyone, emphasising that they will be participating in an AI retrospective. You might say, 'We will run today's retrospective using Appreciative Inquiry. This means focusing on our strengths and successes as a team.' Use the 'Check-in' activity (from *Agile Retrospectives* [DERBY]) with an AI flavour. 'To start our retrospective, I want everyone to think of an adjective that describes something you are proud of on your project. I would like you to share that adjective with everyone.' Go around the team until everyone has spoken.

2. **Generate data** - Brainstorm a series of questions that focus on identifying the team's strengths and successes. Use questions such as, 'If you moved to another team, what practices would you take with you?'; 'Tell us about a time on this project where you felt really good about your work'; 'What do you think is helping us to work effectively as a team?'

3. **Generate insights** - Cluster the information from the previous exercises and ask people to summarise

where key strengths are. Focus people on the potential, and gather answers to questions such as, 'If you could change one thing on this project, what would that be and why?'; 'Imagine that we finished our next iteration delivering all that we promised. What reaction do you think that could have?'; 'Our team is already working well together, how would you describe this team if it were perfect?'

4. **Decide what to do** - Collect the answers and then focus people on generating potential actions that drive the team toward the ideals they identified earlier. Prioritise the actions helping people to connect their actions to their strengths and successes.

5. **Close the retrospective** - Thank people for participating in a different style of retrospective. Use an activity like 'Offer Appreciations' (from *Agile Retrospectives* [DERBY]) to close the retrospective on a positive note.

6.6 Solution-Focused Goal-Driven Retrospectives

My colleague, Jason Yip, has been experimenting with a differently flavoured retrospective format that he calls Solution-Focused, Goal-Driven Retrospectives. Here is his take[3] on this:

'When people think about what's not working,

---

[3]http://jchyip.blogspot.com/2012/02/solution-focused-goal-driven.html

they tend to be in a more negative mood, which then tends to lead to a more narrow perspective... and frankly tends to just be depressing. I first noticed this phenomenon when doing current-state value stream analysis and I suspect the same effect is occurring to a lesser extent with the start of traditional retrospectives. I've begun experimenting with a different style of retrospective inspired by solution-focus[4] and previous goal-driven retrospectives.

This is how he describes the process:

1. **Identify the ideal state/true north/future perfect using the 'Miracle Question'** - 'Imagine that a miracle occurred and all our problems have been solved. How could you tell? What would be different?' The idea here is that we want to make sure everyone is on the same wavelength about where we want to go. Each person works individually using sticky notes. Share and group results into goals. Discuss and resolve differences in vision. This activity would be shorter in subsequent retrospectives as it would be more of a review with adjustments.
2. **Identify where we are now using the 'Scaling Question'** - 'If 10 is the ideal and 0 is where nothing is working, where are we now?' The idea here is to remind people that we are not at 0.

---

[4]http://en.wikipedia.org/wiki/Solution_focused_brief_therapy

3. **Identify what we are already doing that works** - 'What are we already doing that works? That is, why are we [for example] 5 rather than 0?' The idea here is to identify existing resources, strengths, practices that we can leverage for improvement. Each person works individually using sticky notes. Share and group results into resources.

4. **Identify how to move towards the ideal** - 'Using the resources we have, what can we do to move one step closer to 10?' The idea here is to identify the next incremental step to move towards the ideal. Identify actions for each of the goals.

6.7 Dialogue Sheet Retrospectives

Allan Kelly developed Retrospective Dialogue Sheets after a technique invented at the KTH Royal Institute of Technology in Stockholm, Sweden. These sheets are designed to work without the need of a facilitator and are best suited for a small group between 3-8 participants taking between 1-2 hours to complete.

The sheet includes a series of comments, diagrams and questions to prompt discussion and space for participants to write. After printing a large sheet, participants sit around it before following the numbered path to help focus the conversation. Everyone takes an equal number of turns to ask questions, facilitate and make notes on the paper itself.

The team records any observations, comments and thoughts on the sheet, which proves useful when hung on a wall for future reference. The website[5] offers a number of different sheets for different purposes as well as a more detailed guide on how to use each one effectively.

---

[5]http://www.dialoguesheets.com/

7 After the Retrospective

At the end of the retrospective, your team should feel spurred on to implement change. Some participants get a sense of satisfaction from just understanding why an issue came up during the iteration and knowing how to prevent it happening again. Others are rewarded because they feel better informed about whom to approach with questions that were raised but perhaps remain unanswered.

You yourself may notice that issues were raised during this retrospective that you thought the team had acted on previously.

This chapter looks at the responsibilities you will commonly face as a facilitator after a retrospective.

7.1 Capture the Retrospective Output

Retrospectives are meetings that have outcomes and, as with any well-run meeting, some form of notes has to be taken. Unless you have a scribe available, it will fall to you, as facilitator, to capture the retrospective in some way and distribute the output to the participants and possibly key stakeholders.

Before creating a report, determine who might read the report and what they want to do with it. Customise the report to suit the audience. If it is required only by the team to see the actions as output, for example, that's a good minimum, but I would recommend including the outputs from previous activities so the report tells the whole story.

A report for every heartbeat retrospective may seem too frequent at first, but each report is a chapter, if you like, of a bigger story. Each report provides invaluable insights for a retrospective focused on a longer time span, such as a release or an end-of-project retrospective. Use the reports to celebrate the team's progress, overcoming obstacles and embracing continuous improvement.

Use Photos

Take photographs during the retrospectives. Use photographs of the room, participants and of the activities in your report. These visual aids make the report more appealing and easier to digest. The photos also jog participants' recollections of the retrospective and the discussions surrounding the outputs of each retrospective activity.

> NB: Obtain each person's approval if you plan
> to take photos of people. Not everyone likes
> having their photograph taken, especially if it
> is to be distributed to an unknown audience!

For each artefact, briefly describe the process that surrounded its creation rather than just displaying an output. The report should re-tell the story that the team experienced. Consider whether or not it is worth transcribing all of the elements from the sticky notes into the final text of the report.

Consider a Simple Slidedeck

Lightweight infodecks[1] created with slide-presentation software such as Keynote[2] or Powerpoint[3] make great lightweight retrospective reports. A slide's physical dimension enforces readable text size and encourages a focus on key points you want to get across. Slide software simplifies the layout of photos and text and is usually less time-consuming than fiddling with word-processing software or wiki syntax. Most softwares support videos as well. Slides naturally re-create the passage of time, helping you tell a story with the report.

Consider Using a Wiki

Many teams use a wiki to capture information related to the project. This may be the perfect space to write up your notes. Team members can trawl through previous retrospective reports to compare results and find trends, or everyone can add their own personal take to the retrospective report that you initiate. Another advantage of wikis is that you can upload images and movies, although it can be a challenge to make the formatting reasonable without adding a lot of text.

---

[1]http://martinfowler.com/bliki/Infodeck.html

[2]http://www.apple.com/keynote/

[3]http://en.wikipedia.org/wiki/Microsoft_PowerPoint

Include the Prime Directive

A fellow retrospective facilitator, Tim McKinnon taught me to start the report by referring readers to the Prime Directive. The Prime Directive in this context prevents people potentially misinterpreting statements. It might be as simple as:

> 'It is important to view these notes with the retrospective prime directive in mind, [insert the Retrospective Prime Directive Text].'

Add Your Disclaimer

Everyone leaves a retrospective with their own perspective of things. Be aware of this when writing your report. Highlight this distinction to future readers by explaining the context around the notes you record. Be clear that the report reflects your own personal interpretation and offer people a way to correct it if needed. An example you might use follows:

> This retrospective report reflects my interpretation of the discussions held during the meeting on [insert Date]. If you would like to correct an error or make an addition please contact [insert your Name] on [insert appropriate Contact Details].

7.2 Make Actions Visible

Your report captures the essence of the retrospective. If you intend it to prompt people to take actions, don't distribute it by electronic means alone. As the saying goes: 'Out of sight, out of mind'.

Information Radiators[4] or a Team Wall are better ways of making actions constantly visible to the team. Some teams track action items on the board as part of their normal work backlog, making sure that they pull actions through like other tasks. Some teams have a section on the wall dedicated to outstanding actions, including the name of who is currently assigned to each action item, and a due date clearly marked.

As long as your team has healthy habits in keeping the team wall up to date, putting actions on to the wall will make actions more likely to occur.

7.3 Check Actions During Stand-Ups

Many agile teams run a stand-up[5] every day as a way of synchronising and distributing information. The most classic format is asking each participant to share, 'What I did yesterday', 'What I will do today', and 'Any blockers and who I might need help from.' Teams evolve their own

[4]http://alistair.cockburn.us/Information+radiator
[5]http://martinfowler.com/articles/itsNotJustStandingUp.html

ways of running stand-ups such as Walk the Board[6] and asking different questions instead of the original three.

These brief meetings also provide a useful opportunity to check with all action owners for progress, or for those action owners to share progress with the rest of the team. On a larger team (eg. greater than six) I have seen the stand-up work like this:

1. Normal stand-up runs
2. All owners with actions called together post stand-up
3. Any incomplete action is reviewed with the owner to check if the action is still possible and an expected update.

Some teams find running a second, shorter stand-up more effective than running one as a larger group. Calling a second, shorter stand-up often provides more focus, but this format doesn't work if all actions are owned by one individual.

7.4 Actively Chase Action Owners

Agile methods often give the impression of an ideal, self-empowered team - one where everyone uses their initiative and people take actions without reminders. In my career, I have worked on two teams that lived up to this ideal but I

---

[6]http://martinfowler.com/articles/itsNotJustStandingUp.html#WalkTheBoard

can say, hand on heart, that they do not represent the status quo. One reason is that day-to-day activities distract from one-off activities like a particular retrospective action.

Most teams still have some sort of leader - be it a Technical Lead, a Project Manager, or some sort of Iteration Manager/Scrum Master. These people ensure all the little things are kept under control. These roles are often already tasked with making sure that certain activities are carried out, so it naturally falls to them to remind action owners to complete their commitment.

Leaders should not complete the actions themselves. Reminding action owners of their actions already provides tremendous value. More often than not, a simple reminder well before the due date (and the next retrospective) is the best way to ensure actions are completed. Taking time out to chase up actions also offers a good opportunity to discover if there are issues making actions difficult to complete. Team leaders usually have the authority to overcome such issues and to take the steps necessary to progress the action.

7.5 Schedule Follow-Up Sessions

When a team has a lot of issues to deal with, a heartbeat retrospective may not be able to cover them all in sufficient depth. Ask participants if they would like the next retrospective to have a theme focus so that they can explore issues in greater depth.

Some issues are better addressed by the people closest

to them in a one-to-one, before they are addressed by a larger group. After the retrospective, approach the team leaders, point out your observations, and perhaps work with the leaders to book a follow-up session. Consider a technical retrospective where developers can focus more on their own topics.

7.6 Schedule the Next Retrospective

Retrospectives generally match the cadence of the team's iteration or sprint size, so scheduling the next retrospective should be fairly easy. Scheduling the next retrospective may not be feasible if the team is doing kanban[7] and have not agreed on a regular schedule, or if the team is running out of things to discuss. The big issues have been raised, discussed and tackled head on. Smaller issues resolve themselves by the day and the team already celebrates its achievements on a regular basis.

In this case, I would encourage booking in a tentative slot for a retrospective anyway; you can always cancel the booking if it later seems unnecessary. Some teams feel they don't need retrospectives if they don't have any issues; the magic of retrospectives is that they give insights into things you may not have noticed before. If you don't at least create the opportunity for a retrospective, your team could be missing something special.

---

[7]http://en.wikipedia.org/wiki/Kanban_(development)

7.7 Share With Other Teams

Retrospectives generate lots of great ideas and enthusiasm for change. The team that just left your retrospective will benefit significantly from that meeting. Imagine if other teams in your organisation benefited from the same lessons and tried some of those improvements in other areas. Encourage the team to share their retrospective lessons with other people through whatever internal forums, mailing lists or communities exist.

Encourage people to do lunchtime or user-group presentations about the changes the team is making and how well they are working out. What is simple or obvious to one group may not be so obvious to another group. Part of the agile mindset involves continuous learning and helping others to learn. There is nothing more powerful than people talking about their own experiences first hand.

8 Common Retrospective Smells

Even with the best intentions, the right facilitator and ideal conditions, retrospectives are rarely perfect. This section details a number of common retrospective ailments I have seen teams suffer and some preventative action you could take to avoid them.

8.1 All Talk, No Action

I have talked with numerous people who dislike retrospectives, and I think the one thing they had in common was the feeling that the changes promised never happen. They felt that it was all very well talking about problems, what occurred and why, but when they tried to find solutions, the same things came up again and again.

Other facilitators I've spoken to and I have good reasons for holding retrospectives that don't focus exclusively on action items, primarily because they offer a useful arena for different team members to better relate to each other's problems and situations. At the same time, you want to avoid creating situations where participants feel unable to work on their problems or to make any progress.

Regardless of whether problems persist or not, retrospectives are useful for highlighting these problems. Like Information Radiators, retrospectives highlight where pain points lie; they do not make the pain disappear automatically.

The question I ask is: 'What did you do to make the problem go away?', and 'How did you approach fixing your own problems?' I've seen retrospectives where the actions were dependent on people not involved in the retrospective changing external conditions.

Some useful techniques for dealing with this include the Plan of Action, or by allocating enough time to focus explicitly on the 'What next?' steps. Focus on creating actions that team members themselves have the ability to act on. Work on smaller, more specific actions to ensure at least some incremental progress is made. Sometimes that's enough to get things started.

8.2 All Action, No Talk

This is the corollary to the previous All Talk, No Action. A retrospective that focuses too quickly on deciding what to do often ends disastrously, with too many people suggesting different plans of action.

The most common reason behind this scenario is that the team doesn't have a shared view of what happened. A focus on trying to 'take action' often means that everyone sees the problem or status quo differently. This basis means that people naturally have different suggestions to give because they are trying to solve different problems.

There are other downsides to running a retrospective focused purely on 'What do to next?' Sometimes people just need to have their side of the story heard. Retrospectives should provide a safe environment where everyone can be expected to contribute. Team members may see someone differently after listening to them share their part of the story, and perhaps gain a better understanding of someone's motives. Rushing people to suggest actions doesn't allow for this opportunity, which is especially important when teams are fresh to working with each other.

Avoid this anti-pattern by making sure you follow the five stages, dedicating the same length of time to gathering data as to generating insight. Don't rush any of the stages, but do make sure you allow enough time for deciding what to do.

8.3 Conversation Too Controlled

One of the most important points that Kerth, Larsen and Derby all stress in their books is that the facilitator should not have an interest in the conversation. Or, as I heard it succinctly put: 'If you have a point of view to share, you should not be facilitating.' If you break this golden rule, it will have a negative impact on the retrospective. I've seen this happen myself, and it is usually because a person who already holds a position of authority (think project manager, technical or team lead) is facilitating.

> A project manager was running one retro-
> spective I attended. They pointed at people
> to ask them for a single item (what went
> well/less well). They would often drill a per-
> son, insisting on more detail, and then would

comment on their input, along the lines of 'That's a pretty stupid idea,' or 'You really should've done ... instead of ...,' before turning to write the item up on a flip chart. When they had finished, they selected which topics they wanted to discuss further, without involving the group in the decision-making process. I observed, aghast but silent, as people shifted uncomfortably in their seats. They wanted to get their stories out in the open but were afraid it wouldn't lead anywhere productive, and worse, that they might be judged for it.

A facilitator who controls the conversation will often find little valuable output other than meeting their own needs, which is not a healthy situation at all. In my opinion, it's probably wiser to have no retrospective at all than an unhealthy one.

Strategies that I would employ to prevent such a situation include using an independent facilitator (with no vested interest) to run the retrospective; collating input with sticky notes to improve anonymity and efficiency, and spending more time on drawing out the story behind the items to identify any common root causes.

8.4 Too Repetitive

Regular, heartbeat retrospectives become an essential part of the agile team's toolkit. Doing such regular retrospectives inevitably leads to some repetition and it can occasionally get boring for some team members. I can entirely sympathise with being bored by a retrospective; there are any number of reasons why a retrospective might get boring. One might be that no major issues are being raised, to which I would respond by holding the retrospectives less frequently, every fortnight instead of every week, for example.

Another reason might be that the standard format of What Went Well / Less Well (and sometimes Puzzles) becomes predictable and dull.

I list a number of strategies in the next chapter for keeping retrospectives fresh.

8.5 No Preparation

Ever been in a meeting where the organiser doesn't really know why they have brought everyone together, or doesn't even have an agenda to start with? It devalues your time and you feel frustrated.

I've seen the same thing happen when a facilitator hasn't prepared for their retrospective. Preparing well demonstrates respect for participants' time. Preparation doesn't guarantee success, but it certainly means that participants are much more likely to engage, which makes the facilitation a lot easier than it would be otherwise.

One of the main reasons that agile facilitators don't prepare is because they are too busy performing their other day-to-day roles and don't realise they should be putting in the time to prepare.

Facilitators need to be aware that for a retrospective to run well, the facilitator must allocate time to prepare. They need time to plan the session, gather the required materials, set up the room and create the space that will host the retrospective discussions. Use the preparation checklist and make sure you have time to address all of those issues. Whatever you do, don't leave it all until the last minute.

8.6 Too Many Goals

Teams run retrospectives for different reasons. I've found that trying to meet too many goals in a heartbeat retrospective severely limits its effectiveness. When I prepare for retrospectives, one of the first things I do is ask the sponsor (the person who asked me to facilitate) what they want to achieve. Sometimes they don't know themselves, so just asking the question is a useful exercise to get them to clarify their intended goals.

When I've sat in teams new to retrospectives and the goal is not made clear, people bring up too many different issues and it's difficult to resolve anything. One hour seems to be the most that teams are willing to set aside and when you have team issues, technical issues, process issues and more to deal with, the time flies. The result is that nothing gets improved and people get frustrated with the vehicle that brings some visibility (the retrospective).

If you find yourself with too many goals, introduce a limit or a theme to the retrospective. Make this clear at the outset and make sure everyone is okay to proceed on that basis. Using themed retrospectives can be problematic in its own right as you don't get to address issues that lie just outside the theme.

8.7 Poorly Formed Actions

Some teams leave their retrospectives all energised and enthused for change. They take their actions only to look at them later and find that they don't really understand what was intended or that the action is too big to accomplish. At other times, the team members assume that the actions will be dealt with by other team members, and they never get carried out.

Before you leave the retrospective, ensure that actions match up to the SMART qualities previously described. Ask the team if they really think they will be able to complete these actions before the next retrospective and ensure that each one has an explicitly assigned owner.

8.8 One Person Owns All Actions

It's quite common for some teams to come out of a retrospective with only one person - possibly the Technical Lead, Project Manager or Scrum Master - having taken ownership of all the actions. While it's not a problem in itself, if a pattern starts to develop, it creates a sense that change is possible only through a single person with authority, which then makes other team members feel less empowered. This defeats the object of the retrospective.

Work with the group to ensure that ownerships of actions are shared out evenly over a number of retrospectives. Assign two owners to work together on each action so more people are actively involved. Celebrate actions completed by new people at the start of the next retrospective in order to incentivise others to get involved.

9 Keeping Retrospectives Fresh

Even a highly energising, engaging retrospective becomes dull if repeated time and time again. Here are a few practical suggestions that have worked to reinvigorate stagnant sessions and brought new items and points of view to the surface.

9.1 Bring Food

It's amazing how a small box of treats can alter the tone of a retrospective. Sharing meals as a group often brings people closer together. Telling stories while sharing food often creates stronger bonds between members.

Opt for bite-size food, or pre-cut food and avoid foods that require plates or bowls. Bring napkins. The food is there to help stimulate discussions, but shouldn't distract people from the main activities. In my experience, when people first bring food to retrospectives they usually bring sweets, chocolate bars, tiny cakes, biscuits or crisps because these foods are widely regarded as treats. Try to vary the types of food you bring, not forgetting the healthy options. Bring fruit such as grapes, apples or pears or dried mango or apricots, for example, or a bag of nuts or muesli bars. Try to take into account any special dietary needs or allergies that the team may have. Strict vegetarians can't eat gelatine, for example, which rules out many sweets.

Encourage people to bring food for sharing at the next

retrospective. Sharing food builds relationships and often leads to better conversations.

9.2 Ask Different Questions

As I have mentioned before, the most popular format for a retrospective starts by asking the three questions 'What went well?', 'What went less well?' and 'What still puzzles us?' These three questions form a powerful combination that draws out plenty of information. Used too often, however, these questions can get tedious.

Asking essentially the same question in different words is effective in changing the tone of the retrospective and keeps it engaging for participants. Combining the questions with a metaphor supported by a visual guide such as a diagram on a whiteboard or flip chart helps people think about things from a slightly different perspective, often adding to the discussion.

Variants you might try include:

- **Anchors and Engines** - Draw a speedboat and ask, 'What anchors may be dragging you down?' and 'What engines are helping you accelerate?'
- **Hot Air Balloon** - Draw a hot air balloon, asking, 'What things are acting as sandbags, slowing you down?' and 'What things are helping you move upwards?'
- **Train** - Draw a picture of a train, asking 'What cargo may be slowing the train down?' and 'What sort of fuel is helping the train go faster?'

9.3 Run an Energiser

If your retrospective goes on for longer than an hour or is held directly after lunch, you may experience an energy slump. When this happens, facilitators can run a short activity (say 5-10 minutes) designed to get people on their feet, to get the blood flowing after a heavy lunch and more ready to contribute to the session at hand. These activities are appropriately called 'Energisers'.

It's easy to find ideas on the internet if you search using the terms 'energisers', 'ice-breakers', and 'warm-up games'. Look for activities that will get people out of their chairs; make people use more than their hands and try games that are designed to engage parts of the brain that aren't exercised in the fact-hunting and evaluation session ahead.

> **Who am I?** is an energiser where everyone stands in a circle. Write the names of famous people on to large (3"x5") index cards, one name per card. Tape a card on to the back of each participant. The object of the exercise is for each person to discover the identity taped to their back by asking questions that can be answered only with 'Yes' or 'No'. Give everyone two minutes to walk around asking questions of the other participants. At the end of the two minutes, ask everyone to stand in a circle and ask each person to guess their own identity. Then allow each person to compare their guess with the name they actually had

on their back.

Avoid exercises that pit people against each other in sub groups as this may exacerbate any ill or awkward situations that are already present. Try to avoid exercises that may make people too uncomfortable, or are physically difficult and dangerous for your environment. Don't be afraid to push the boundaries a little, but be sensitive to the team you have.

9.4 Vary the Activities

You've run retrospectives iteration after iteration and even though you vary the questions people still seemed to run out of enthusiasm. It's not necessarily that people have run out of things to say, it's just that participants already know what is coming. Introduce one new exercise per retrospective to keep insights fresh. Look for exercises that the team hasn't used before, or try creating a new retrospective exercise yourself. Be sure to write it up and share it with the community.

Limit new exercises to one per retrospective. Varying things too much may throw people; they could start wondering about there are so many changes instead of focusing on being a participant and contributing their part of the story.

Even if you don't vary the exercises, consider varying the way that you facilitate the discussion and look for different techniques. One exercise that I like to pull out every so often is the Fishbowl Discussion.

Fishbowl Discussion

Purpose: To provide a fast-moving conversation for a large group. **Set-up**: Five chairs set up as an inner circle, facing inwards; the rest are set up as an outer circle, also facing inwards. **Method**:

1. Ask for four people (who will seed the discussion) to sit in four of the five chairs. Only the people sitting in these chairs are allowed to speak.
2. Explain that one (and only one) chair must always be empty within the fishbowl.
3. Explain that anyone in the outer circle, whose view is not being represented in the discussion may sit inside the fishbowl and offer to give their own. Of course, this means someone inside the fishbowl must leave.

Only those in the fishbowl may speak, but as a facilitator, you may encourage people to join the fishbowl, and that encourages someone to leave. Over time, the original participants in the fishbowl should change. If one person in particular never volunteers to leave the fishbowl, as a facilitator, you may propose that that person leaves. Another alternative is to ask for the entire fishbowl to empty out and allow a completely fresh set of people to occupy it.

9.5 Change the Environment

Most buildings don't have many meeting rooms and you probably have to book the only one that will fit everyone comfortably for the retrospective. If this is the case, you will find that people start to automatically head to the same seats when they enter; they develop a habit. This isn't necessarily bad in itself, but it could be if their habit is to slump into their chair with a slightly glazed expression. Your job as a facilitator is to keep the retrospective as fresh and engaging as possible.

Consider switching room if possible to keep the surroundings different. If alternative rooms are not available, change the room layout and the way participants sit. Consider setting it up in mirror form so that when people enter, it looks familiar but different. Or arrange the chairs differently, or even ask participants to swap seats during the retrospective. Each of these tiny details, however insignificant it may seem, can really help a participant to discover a fresh perspective.

9.6 Appeal To Other Skillsets

If you're running an agile retrospective, you probably produce some kind of software. If so, a large proportion of your job probably entails working with the written and spoken word. We have many more skills than just writing and reading or listening and speaking. Triggering the use of other skills helps participants feel more immersed in the retrospective experience and I often find the conversations and discussions are much richer as a result. Encourage people to get up and walk around during the retrospective and to use their hands as well as their eyes to inspect others' work.

Ensure that what activities you do are not biased towards the skills you use every day. Look for manual activities that require people to build, draw, paint or construct a visual model of some sort. Seek activities that require abstraction, metaphor and storytelling. One example that I like is the simple **Weather Report** activity.

> **Weather Report** - Ask participants to describe how the last sprint went in terms of the weather. Some people might use one-word answers like 'Sunny', but occasionally people really tap into their creativity (indeed the point!) and give an extended response. For example: 'We had a series of sunny spells amid the presence of dark clouds threatening rain. I definitely heard some thunder in the distance. We were lucky to have avoided the bad storm, though forecasts tell us we may not yet be in the clear.'

9.7 Make It Less Formal

I've been part of retrospectives in all sorts of environments, from casual start-up, working out of a converted house, all the way up to your corporate banking environment. Something definitely shifts, the closer you get to a more 'corporate' environment, which makes retrospectives go stale quicker than they would in a start-up environment.

Perhaps it's the way that people dress as well as the corporate culture that makes conversations more stilted?

Either way, as a facilitator, do anything you can to make the retrospective appear less like a formal meeting. Think about asking people to leave their jackets at their desks, or include an activity that involves some informal play to break the corporate atmosphere.

I keep the Art Gallery activity from *Project Retrospectives* in my pocket for occasions such as this. Ask participants to think back to the last iteration and to draw a picture that summarises their feelings about how it went. Given a short time limit and the average person's drawing abilities, most pictures end up being rather abstract, made up of circles, boxes and lines with the occasional stick figure.

Putting the pictures up around the room helps to make the retrospective less formal.

10 Concluding

Retrospectives offer you and your team a safe haven for introspection and often prove to be a catalyst for change. When done right, retrospectives give endless insight and help teams rally around continuous improvement.

10.1 Powerful Results

Your retrospectives are most powerful if you do the following:

1. **When Planning** - Identify the purpose for the retrospective, set the agenda and plan well, allowing enough time for the retrospective activities. Reserve an appropriate place, gather enough materials and ensure the right participants turn up on time. Before the participants arrive, prepare the space by laying out materials and ensuring all equipment works as expected.

2. **In the Retrospective** - Focus on independent facilitation and ensure the group moves through the retrospective framework at the same pace. Focus conversations on fact-finding before uncovering root causes. Focus on concrete actions only after the group has identified the root causes. Make action items more likely to happen by assigning action owners and shaping them to fit the SMART criteria.

3. **The Follow Up** - Write up your retrospective notes and include photos where possible. Keep the action

items as visible as possible and actively chase action owners to ensure change happens. The true value of a retrospective is only realised when change happens as a result of the discussions.

10.2 Constant Change

If I had to pick the most important agile practice out of all, retrospectives would be my number one. With the retrospective practice, you can evolve your way to excel in any situation.

If I have done what I set out to do, the advice in this book will make your retrospectives even better. Let me know if this book helped you, and help me make this book even better by submitting feedback to me. You can contact me via twitter on @patkua[1] or leave a comment on the book's website[2]. I look forward to hearing your stories about how retrospectives have helped your teams succeed.

---

[1]http://twitter.com/patkua
[2]http://leanpub.com/the-retrospective-handbook

Appendix A: Retrospective Activities

Books

- Derby, E., D. Larsen and K. Schwaber, 2006: *Agile Retrospectives: Making Good Teams Great.* Pragmatic Bookshelf.
- Kerth, N.L., 2001: *Project Retrospectives: A Handbook for Team Reviews.* Dorset House Publishing.
- Hohmann, L., 2006: *Innovation Games: Creating Breakthrough Products Through Collaborative Play,* Addison-Wesley Professional.

Websites

- Agile Retrospective Resource Wiki[3] - A wiki site dedicated to the retrospective practice including example exercises, tips and tricks and useful advice from the public.
- Agile Tips[4] - Paulo Caroli is a colleague who I know is passionate about retrospectives. He writes about his experiences and attempts with different exercises on his website.
- Diana Larsen's Blog[5] - Diana Larsen expands on activities not yet covered in her book.

---

[3]http://agileretrospectivewiki.org/
[4]http://agiletips.com/
[5]http://www.futureworksconsulting.com/blog/category/retrospectives/

- Skycoach on Retrospectives[6] - I collaborated with Nick Oostvogels on a retrospective workshop and found another practitioner trying new exercises and writing frequently about them on his blog.
- Mark Levison on Agile Retrospectives[7] - Mark writes a good introductory article and often publishes links to other agile-related materials including retrospectives.
- Patterns for Iteration Retrospectives[8] - An old but still particularly relevant page on effective retrospectives patterns from Extreme Programming Explored author William C. Wake.
- Resources on Retrospectives[9] by Brad Appleton - A good collection of links pointing to other web resources related to retrospectives.

---

[6]http://skycoach.be/category/continuous-improvement/

[7]http://agilepainrelief.com/notesfromatooluser/2010/05/agile-retrospectives.html

[8]http://xp123.com/articles/patterns-for-iteration-retrospectives/

[9]http://bradapp.blogspot.com/2009/07/resources-on-retrospectives.html

Appendix B: Resources to Becoming a Better Facilitator

Facilitation Resources

- Bens, I., 2000: *Facilitating with Ease: Core Skills for Facilitators, Team Leaders and Members, Managers, Consultants, and Trainers*, Jossey-Bass.
- Bens, I., 2005: *Advanced Facilitation Strategies: Tools and Techniques to Master Difficult Situations*, Jossey-Bass.
- Kaner, S., L. Lind, C. Toldi, S. Fisk and D. Berger, 2007: *Facilitator's Guide to Participatory Decision-Making*, John Wiley & Sons.
- Kline, N. 1998: *Time to Think: Listening to Ignite the Human Mind*, Cassell Illustrated.
- Schwartz, R., 2002: *The Skilled Facilitator*, Jossey Bass.
- Tabaka, J. 2006: *Collaboration Explained: Facilitation Skills for Software Project Leaders*, Addison-Wesley Professional.
- Stanfield, B.R. 2000: *The Art of Focused Conversations*. New Society Publishers.

Resources on Related Topics

The previous list shows books that will probably be most relevant to you as a facilitator. There are a few related books that help to round out the skills of a facilitator.

- Deutsch, M., P.T. Coleman, E.C. Marcus (eds.), 2006: *The Handbook of Conflict Resolution: Theory and Practice*, Jossey-Bass.
- Fisher, R., W. Ury and B. Patton, 1991: *Getting to Yes: Negotiating Agreement Without Giving In*, Random House Business.
- Gottman, J.M. and N. Silver, 1999: *The Seven Principles for Making Marriage Work*, Crown.
- Noonan, B., 2007: *Discussing the Undiscussable: A Guide To Overcoming Defensive Routines in the Workplace*, Jossey-Bass.
- Patterson, K., J. Grenny, R. McMillan and A. Switzler, 2002: *Crucial Conversations: Tools for Talking When Stakes are High*. McGraw-Hill Professional.
- Patterson, K., J. Grenny, R. McMillan and A. Switzler, 2004: *Crucial Confrontations: Tools for resolving broken promises, violated expectations, and bad behavior*, McGraw-Hill Professional.
- Stoltzfus, T., 2008: *Coaching Questions: A Coach's Guide to Powerful Asking Skills*, Pegasus Creative Arts.
- Ury, W., 1991: *Getting Past No: Negotiating With Difficult People*, Random House Business.

Appendix C: References

The following section lists books, articles and papers referenced throughout this book.

- [COOPE] Cooperrider, D.L. and D. Whitney, 2005: *A Positive Revolution in Change: Appreciative Inquiry.* Berrett-Koehler.

- [DEBON] De Bono, E., , 1992: *Six Action Shoes.* HarperCollins Publishers.

- [DERBY] Derby, E., D. Larsen and K. Schwaber, 2006: *Agile Retrospectives: Making Good Teams Great.* Pragmatic Bookshelf.

- [ELSASH] Elashoff, J.D. and R.E. Snow, 1971: *Pygmalion reconsidered; a case study in statistical inference: reconsideration of the Rosenthal-Jacobson data on teacher expectancy,* Charles A. Jones Publishing Company.

- [HOFST] Hofstede, G., 2001: *Culture's Consequences: Comparing Values, Behaviors, Institutions, and Organizations Across Nations,* Sage Publications.

- [KANER] Kaner, S., L. Lind, C. Toldi, S. Fisk and D. Berger, 2007: *Facilitator's Guide to Participatory Decision-Making,* John Wiley & Sons.

- [KERTH] Kerth, N.L., 2001: *Project Retrospectives: A Handbook for Team Reviews.* Dorset House Publishing.

- [LENCI] Lencioni, P., 2002: *The Five Dysfunctions of a Team: A Leadership Fable*, Jossey-Bass.

- [MARGO] Margoli, A., 1993: Tips for Trainers: The Margolis Wheel. *Participatory Learning and Action* 17. http://www.planotes.org/documents/plan_01713.PDF

- [SENGE] Senge, P., 1990: *The Fifth Discipline: The Art and Practice of the Learning Organization.* Doubleday.

- [ROSEN] Rosenthal, R. and L. Jacobson, 1992: *Pygmalion in the Classroom: Teacher Expectation and Pupils' Intellectual Development.* Irvington Publishers.

- [TUCKM] Tuckman, B.W. 1965: Developmental sequence in small groups. *Psychological Bulletin* **63**(6): 384-99.

3048928R00074

Printed in Great Britain
by Amazon.co.uk, Ltd.,
Marston Gate.